which?
essential guides

D1386399

D

YC

" Whether you are updating your heating system or having a new kitchen fitted, the time and costs involved in making improvements to your property should not be underestimated. This book has been written to show you how to do exactly this, to help ensure your project – no matter how small or large – is successful. **"**

Kate Faulkner

About the author

Kate Faulkner has written extensively on property and is the author of two other Which? Essential Guides – *Renting and Letting* and *Buy, Sell and Move House*. As well as writing on the subject, Kate has bought and renovated property for many years and has worked in the industry for over ten – her website, www.designsonproperty.co.uk, provides help to those buying and selling property in the UK. Kate lives in Nottingham.

essential guides

DEVELOP
YOUR PROPERTY

KATE FAULKNER

Which? Books are commissioned and published by Which? Ltd,
2 Marylebone Road, London NW1 4DF

Books: Angela Newton
Project management for Which? Books Luke Black
email: books@which.co.uk

Distributed by Littlehampton Book Services Ltd, Faraday Close, Durrington, Worthing,
West Sussex BN13 3RB

British Library Cataloguing in Publication Data
A catalogue record for this publication is available from the British Library

Copyright © Which? Ltd 2007

ISBN 978 1 84490 038 1

Although the author and publishers endeavour to make sure the information
in this book is accurate and up-to-date, it is only a general guide. Before taking action
on property improvement, financial, legal, or medical matters you should consult a
qualified professional adviser, who can consider your individual circumstances. The author
and publishers cannot accordingly accept liability for any loss or damage suffered as a
consequence of relying on the information contained in this guide.

Author's acknowledgements
This book would not have been possible without the help and support from the following
people and their companies/organisations: Mark Spurling at RBS Associates, Barry Turner
from LABC, Jeff Emms from Potton, Kevin Reed from Eurocell, Anne Taylor and Diane
Hewitt from Notts CC, David, Caroline and Tim from CORGI , Joanne Morris from IHPE,
Brendan OConnor from RIBA, Diane Dale from CIAT, Andrew Thomas from Aitchison
Rafferty, Kieran (my electrician!) and William DIYNot and Gary from Broadoakbuildings.
Thanks, too, to Emma and Sean Callery and Luke and Angela from Which?.

Edited by: Emma Callery
Designed by: Bob Vickers
Index by: Lynda Swindells
Cover photographs by: Alamy
Printed and bound by Scotprint, Scotland

For a full list of Which? Books, please call 01903 828557, access our website at
www.which.co.uk, or write to Littlehampton Book Services.
For other enquiries call 0800 252 100.

Contents

Introduction

For most people in the UK, the property they own or have equity in is their biggest asset. Approximately 30 per cent of people own their home outright and, of those, some 40 per cent have an average mortgage of £120,000. And British people like to own property abroad, too, with over 250,000 UK households owning a second property overseas.

Property as an asset is increasingly seen as an important part of an individual's retirement plan. Some people may want to invest in changes to their property now, to maximise its value later. Others may choose to sell and buy a bigger home, hoping its value will increase, or in retirement, downsize to a smaller, less expensive home that is mortgage free.

If adding or at least maintaining the value of your home is important to you, then it is just as important to ensure these changes fit in with what the property owning public want. If changes are quirky or expensive to maintain, such as swimming pools, then this can reduce the value of the all-important property asset.

" Property as an asset is increasingly seen as an important part of an individual's retirement plan - investing in changes now, maximises its value later. "

When considering what changes to make to your home, don't assume that what was acceptable several years ago, is still acceptable now. There are currently a number of changes to the law that affect what you can and cannot do to a property yourself, and what requires professional assistance. Ten years ago, you could do pretty much anything to your home, except, perhaps, a major extension, which required planning permission, or working on a gas supply. Now, however, there are rules and regulations on electrical work, the types of windows you can have and the energy efficiency of your property. The end result is that if you don't get work approved when required, it can reduce the value of your property when you try to sell.

In today's environment, it is also important to be aware that once you decide you would like to go ahead with a project, many of the really good professionals may be booked up for work well in advance. Back in the 1990s, when property was not a 'booming' market and we were in recession, finding a builder, plumber or electrician wasn't too difficult. Now, however, fewer people have been entering these professions and many prefer to work on commercial, new-build projects or are kept busy by the new buy-to-let investors who use them to maintain their 1.7 million properties! Depending on which area you live in, it can take several weeks to a year or more to secure a contractor who is available and has a good reputation. This gives 'cowboys' a real chance to take advantage of those who choose not to wait. Problems can then arise, such as taking your money and disappearing with it before they have finished the work, or producing poor quality work, which costs yet more to get fixed when it goes wrong. Poor work on a property is always likely to be spotted by a surveyor when selling and can even result in your buyer pulling out of the sale.

In the UK, over £17 billion are spent on home improvement projects every year. Many of these do add value to a home, but with an aging property stock, many people are spending money on projects that may make the property look better on a day-to-day basis, but actually do little to ensure that the property is waterproof and well looked after.

Most people don't realise that for their insurance policy to be valid, this often requires a property to be well maintained. For example, many buildings insurance policies require that you alert them to any major structural changes to a property. If you check the small print of your buildings and contents insurance, keeping them in 'good repair' is essential for a valid claim. If the insurance company can prove that the damage you are claiming for was due to poor maintenance, then they may not pay out, costing you more money in the long run than it would have done to get it fixed.

In short, with property being such an important investment; the changing regulations and difficulties working with contractors; and the responsibility to insurance companies to keep property in a good state of repair, it is wise to gain all the help and information you can before you start your dream improvements.

‟When you are selling your property, a surveyor is likely to spot if work on it is poor, which could result in your buyer pulling out. ”

MAKE A LIST

Start by making a list of all the things you like and dislike about your home. It is also a good idea to think of what you like about friends' and family's homes, too. This helps focus your thoughts on what changes could be made to improve your living accommodation.

Initially, you might think that the only change you need is a new kitchen or bathroom. When you sit down and think about what you really want, you may prefer to create a kitchen diner with double doors to the garden. You may also be able to add an en suite at the same time as upgrading your bathroom for only a few thousand pounds more. The increased costs of these changes might be minimal, but they could help add value to your home's sale price and, more importantly, make a substantial change to your enjoyment and use of your home.

If you are looking at making major changes, such as a two-storey extension or a loft conversion, it may be worth double-checking to see if selling your current home and buying another could achieve what you want at the same cost or less. However, bear in mind that with the increased cost of stamp duty for properties over £250,000 together with the general increase in property value and estate agent charges, the costs of moving over the last five years have substantially increased. Just make sure that you consider all the costs involved in moving and any on-going increase in payments, such as council tax and heating bills, and compare these to the costs of improvement (see box, pages 33). If you are considering paying out thousands of pounds on home improvements, check how much it would cost to sell and buy a property that would provide the space you need and compare the difference.

Once you have your list of everything that you want to change about your property, decide which are the 'must have changes' and those that you would like to make. It is much better to brief an architect, builder or kitchen planner on all the things you want and then cut back, than to add things halfway through. Even worse would be to wish that at the end of the project you had built a two-storey rather than a single-storey extension.

❝ Would it be better to sell up and buy another property? ❞

The costs of buying and selling a home in the UK		
	2002	2007
Property price	£150,000	£255,000
Estimated cost of buying/selling	£ 6,000	£ 16,000

VALUE FOR MONEY

Next, think through how long you are likely to stay in the property after the changes. This will influence how much you spend on the project and what quality of materials and labour you invest in. For example, if you are improving your home because you want to sell it and maximise the sale price, then spending money on the most expensive materials may not be the best idea as you might not get your money back. However, if you are updating a kitchen or bathroom and intend to stay in the property for more than ten years, investing in more expensive, lifetime guaranteed materials may mean that over time you get your money back.

Many people make improvements to a property without considering whether they will add value or not, or worse still, believing they will, when in reality they could even devalue a property. There are some things that, done well, are almost sure to add value and these are typically ones that add space, such as a bedroom. 'Improvements' that are bespoke features to a property, such as a sauna or outdoor swimming pool, generally won't add value.

As it is your home, as long as you own it outright, or get approval from the mortgage lender (where necessary) and stay within the laws of the land, it is entirely up to you what you do. However,

it is good practice to check with the local estate agent or the surveyor that originally assessed your property's value as to what change in value and saleability the improvements may make. This can save you from making serious mistakes and in some cases the agent/surveyor might give you ideas from other properties they have seen, which might save you money or help further improve the property's value.

❝ Some improvements can actually devalue a property. ❞

The 'ceiling' price

It is important to know that spending money on things that usually improve the value of a home, doesn't always pay back. For example, spending £20,000 on a kitchen doesn't mean your property value will immediately increase by £20,000. Every property has a 'ceiling' price according to its location, size and age. So if most properties in the road sell for £150,000 and you spend £20,000 on a kitchen and bathroom, it is unlikely you will get more than £150,000 for the property. Unless you are genuinely not worried about making a return on the improvements, ensure that you don't spend more on the property than you could gain on the sale price.

 For more information about planning a kitchen or bathroom that ensures you make a return on the improvement, see pages 116–26.

ADDING VALUE

It is easy to get carried away with a new kitchen, bathroom or conservatory while neglecting other areas of a property. For example, if you have a roof that is leaking and is causing damp walls and rotting the timbers, it is important to make sure these essential repairs are done first. Otherwise they will cost you more in the long run and may make your new improvements worthless.

The following three basic 'rules of thumb' will help to at least maintain, and hopefully add value to, your home:

- Fixing a problem that is/would cause long-term damage to the property.
- Adding additional space/rooms.
- Updating the property to a popular look and feel.

Home improvements made in 2006

Rank	Room	Number of people (%)
1	Kitchen	29
2	Double glazing	8
3	Conservatory	8
4	Extension/extra rooms	7
5	Central heating	6

Home improvements rated by Halifax valuers

Rank	Room	Rank out of ten
1	Loft conversion	10
2=	New kitchen	8
2=	Painting and decorating	8
4=	Extension/extra rooms	7
4=	New bathroom	7

In 2006, Halifax conducted a major survey on the types of home improvement people carried out, and how these were rated by valuers (see the two tables, opposite). Interestingly, what people think adds value to a home and what actually adds value is not necessarily the same thing.

By making improvements according to the second table, you would hopefully at least get your money back and may well add to the value of your home.

Key to this is developing a home to fit into the lifestyle that people are looking for, but making this flexible in case trends change at a later date. For example, most garages are currently used for storage as opposed to housing a car. What most people are more interested in is a further bedroom, particularly with an en suite, or creating an office space or a 'second sitting room'. From a parking perspective, all they usually care about is that there is somewhere for a car to be parked off the road. Adding extra space to a property in this way can increase the value between 5 and 10 per cent.

Kitchens and bathrooms

Kitchens and bathrooms are an important addition to a property's value as long as you spend an average amount rather than splash out on the equivalent of a

Greek spa when the property is only worth £100,000. Fitting a good quality new kitchen and bathroom can add 10 per cent to the property's value, particularly if it fits in either with the character of the property – for example, a Victorian house – or with the latest trends, such as granite surfaces, self-shutting and deep and wide drawers, or drop-down televisions.

The garden

Finally, when looking at adding value, many people forget that a family friendly, easy-to-maintain garden can now add approximately 15 per cent to a property's value. Again, it needs to be in keeping with the type of property and its ceiling value. Even if you only have a small concrete courtyard, you can still enhance its look and appeal with a few well-placed flowerpots and a small water feature.

❝ The key to developing a home is to fit into the lifestyle people currently seek, while making it flexible in case trends change later on. ❞

 See pages 187–98 for advice on garden improvements and see pages 116–26 for kitchens and bathrooms.

11

LOOKING TO THE FUTURE

When looking at home improvements, it is important to be aware of how future rules and regulations may change. For example, it is increasingly important to make our homes as energy efficient as possible. Not only because the cost of power is likely to continue to increase, but also because changes in the law require each home to be assessed with an Energy Performance Certificate, which will be required by law for anyone selling a home from August 2007. If you ever need or plan to rent out your property, you will also need a gas and preferably an electrical safety certificate that states you have the most economical type of heating and that it is serviced annually.

Home Information Packs

These will be introduced from August 2007 and will include some of the legal documentation on the property's title deeds and what changes may be being made locally that could affect the property. It will also include an energy performance certificate, which assesses how the property performs from a heating and ventilation perspective and will be given ratings (a bit like some white goods have) on the property's energy efficiency.

WHAT TO CONSIDER CAREFULLY

While adding space typically does add value, it is possible to lose value or lessen the appeal of your property to future buyers if you extend a property. For example, there are many properties that are four- or five-bedroomed family homes, but have little or no garden space and even nowhere to park a car. As a result, a property like this is difficult for families to live with on a day-to-day basis.

It is also possible to over extend a property in one area, such as the ground floor, which ends up creating an unbalanced home and this can cause a price conflict with buyers. For example, imagine a huge five-bedroomed property with a beautiful large garden. All the rooms are well proportioned and the property is large enough for a family to expand and grow up without ever moving again. However, there is one major flaw that makes the property much less attractive to a family. The kitchen is a small galley kitchen and the washing machine and dishwasher have to be housed in the adjoining garage as there is no room in the kitchen area.

There is also a difference between what 'wish' lists people have for living in a property and the real value that these enhancements have when selling it. In addition to the Halifax survey results

 For more information about home information packs, see the *Which? Essential Guide Buy, Sell and Move House.*

given on page 10, a recent survey from Abbey Bank suggests that the top five home improvement 'wish list' items are:

- Gadgets, such as flat screen TVs and automatic lighting.
- A jacuzzi, hot tub or sauna.
- A swimming pool.
- A roof terrace or balcony.
- A gym.

Although we may wish for them when asked in a survey, these are not necessarily things that truly add value when it comes to selling a home. This is mainly due to the fact that the cost of up-keep is too much and that few people would purchase a property because it has a gym if it meant the bathroom had to be downstairs. Indeed, many estate agents dread a property that has a swimming pool or sauna, or any other addition that is expensive to maintain. Large, expensive properties in beautiful surroundings can cope with this as an expense, but in an average three- or four-bed house, when it comes to buying a property, it is more hassle than it is worth. You should consider a quicker, cheaper and potentially more sociable option of joining the local leisure centre or health club!

Finally, bespoke and personalised features that reduce a property's mass appeal do little to enhance a property's value. Examples of this are garish colours and other decoration on the walls, ceilings or floors, and stained-glass windows that aren't in keeping with the property's type and age. Similarly, removing in-keeping character features, such as fireplaces, dado rails and the original floor tiles from an old property and replacing them with a more modern look and feel, is not conducive to a quick sale. Many people who purchase an old property pay a premium for the privilege, as a result they expect to see at least some of the original features.

66 Many estate agents dread trying to sell a property with an addition that is expensive to maintain, such as a swimming pool or sauna. 99

Whatever rules of thumb you choose to follow or flout, if you intend to stay for ten years or more, then it is up to you as to whether you make the changes or not – as long as you are not expecting someone else to cover the cost in the future. The one rule that you should not ignore is making changes to a property that may mean a mortgage company won't lend. For example, if you

If you are planning on selling your property after you've developed it, bear in mind that neutral decorations can make all the difference to a quick sale - for more advice, see pages 158-62.

want to borrow from your mortgage for the improvements, they are unlikely to lend to you if they don't believe that the property will be worth the additional loan after the changes have been made. The lender will also want to be reassured that any structural changes to a property are properly supported and may even require a further survey – at your cost – to be sure that the property is still worth the money they have lent you.

If in any doubt about the merits of the property improvements you are making, ask the opinion of a local surveyor or estate agent to be sure you are making the most of your money. Remember to always check with your mortgage lender that they are happy to approve what you are doing. However, many property improvements do add great value to a home, not just financially, but also for the lifestyle you live. They are definitely worth considering versus moving home and there is nothing like the feeling when the job is done and you can sit back and enjoy your new home.

“ If you are not sure about the merits of property improvements, ask for the opinion of a local surveyor or estate agent. ”

Understanding your home

When it comes to improving a property, the first thing to do is to understand how your home is constructed. Some houses easily offer extra space, others don't. In this chapter we describe the key differences and what to watch out for in your home improvement project.

Property construction

The UK has one of the richest and most diverse ranges of properties in the world – from medieval castles to Tudor mansions. Although many of these are now gone, over 50 per cent of our property stock is still more than 50 years old, leaving homeowners with high on-going maintenance costs, let alone the opportunity to spend money improving it.

When looking at any property improvement it is helpful, and in some cases essential, to understand the age and type of property together with the key features of its construction. This will have a huge impact on your choice of property improvement and the cost. For example, if you want to add an extra room, depending on the construction of your roof, it may be better to add the extra space as a loft conversion as opposed to an extension.

In many cases, when considering a major structural change to your property, or anything to do with plumbing and wiring, you are likely to have to secure professional help. This may be in the form of a surveyor, architect or an assessment from a plumber or electrician. However, if you know the age of your property and have a good look around,

with the help of the information below and professional advice you should be able to save some time and money working out what is and isn't possible from a structural and cost perspective.

❝ It can be essential to understand the type of property and how it was constructed. This can have a huge impact on the options and costs. ❞

 Choosing and employing contractors to provide you with professional help is a skill – see pages 78-102 for advice.

18TH CENTURY AND BEFORE

Properties built in this era are always likely to cost more to renovate and improve than any other. The main reason being that there were no regulations with regard to a property's construction, so any improvement is likely to require some upgrading to meet the current standards. You may also need to employ an architect, builder and even a surveyor or other contractor who has specialist skills and experience in renovating old properties, and you will need to consider buying more expensive materials to maintain its look and feel.

Old properties tend to have a very individual construction as they were built from whatever the surrounding area could supply. For example, many properties are built of local stone, such as cobbles or slate. Where timber was in abundance, they may have been mainly built with a timber frame, a form of construction still popular today. The roof structure is likely to be timber frame and overlaid with locally resourced thatch, clay, slate or other materials. The stone or timber frame of the property was often fixed together with whatever was available in the region (clay or mud) and sometimes mixed with other materials, such as straw.

Initially, if you are looking to extend, build up or underneath the property, you need to check that the damp-proof course is in good order, and what, if any, foundations the property has. This is likely to require a professional inspection from a surveyor, structural engineer and/or damp specialist. If you are considering a loft extension, this will depend on the height of the roof space and its construction. You are likely to require some reinforcement of the property to ensure it is safe to bear the load of a new room.

❝ You may need to employ people with specialist skills and experience working with old properties. ❞

Electrics and heating

Any additions or changes to the electrics and heating are likely to be more expensive than for properties built later – and more restrictive. For example, the ceilings and walls are unlikely to have anywhere to hide or run the wires and pipes, so they may need to be hidden behind beams, in trunking or purpose-made boxing. It may even be difficult to incorporate things such as spot lighting as you can't sink them into ceilings where there is no 'space' between it and the upstairs floor.

17

PRE 1930S

Many Victorian and some Edwardian properties were built during this period as the population expanded rapidly. Changes to production and transport made bricks easier and more cost-effective to build with. The roof structure is likely to be a large, strong timber frame and the walls would normally be built from brick on the outer and supporting (or load-bearing) walls, with lathe and plaster on the walls partitioning the rooms.

Foundations were usually a 'footing course', which included a trench being dug out, perhaps filled with rubble and then a brick foundation. In these days, damp-proof courses didn't exist, so it's important when renovating to check that one has been put in, is still in guarantee and working effectively.

Finally, any plumbing, gas supply and wiring work in an old property can open a can of worms. Usually older properties are upgraded over time in lots of different ways, so unless the property has been rewired and re-plumbed in the last one or two years, you should be aware that major improvements are likely to be needed on the electrics and plumbing to bring them up to the required standards.

1930S TO 1980S

Since the 1930s, the construction of property has been regulated by local councils. Properties built in the 1930s were usually of brick construction with a cavity wall to aid insulation, especially on the ground floor. However, because this restricted the patterns that the bricklayer could create, they were often not extended to the first floor, instead many retained the solid brick wall structure of the Victorian age.

The roof structure was timber frame with a covering of tiles, which may have been made of slate, clay or even cement. The foundations are likely to have been a sturdy, 'concrete strip foundation' (see page 20). Concrete was used as the bed of the foundation while the old Victorian ways were maintained with a double thickness of brick until the property was out of the ground.

Properties built since the Second World War have been a real mixture of construction methods. In the 1950s, they continued to be built in a similar way to 1930s properties. In the 1960s and 70s, though, new techniques and materials were used, such as 'brick and block' and there was a huge increase in the use of cement. Many of the covering materials used during this time have not proved to be as strong as those used in previous years.

 It is likely that the foundations were only good enough for one storey, so if you are adding more weight either by a second storey or sometimes a loft conversion, you may need to underpin the property.

The foundations would have been built down to approximately 1–1.5m and are likely to be made of concrete, much like the strip foundations for 1930s properties. Load-bearing walls would have been of brick and block, and internal walls would have been stud (or partition) walls.

The roof structure would be of a sawn timber frame construction, which would have been crafted by a carpenter on-site, using felt and tiles to cover and waterproof the property. During this time, flat roofs were introduced, which are not usually built to cope with the weight of a second storey, or indeed a roof terrace. Be aware that these usually last approximately 10–15 years, so if you are improving a room or the area around a flat roof, make sure that it doesn't require re-roofing and understand any structural changes required for an upward extension.

❝Some modern buildings are built to allow for future improvement, such as loft conversions or two-storey extensions.❞

1980S TO PRESENT DAY

Many properties built since the 1980s are of either brick and timber frame or brick and block construction, with load-bearing walls being made from brick blocks and plastered over. Internal walls are likely to be stud walls with plaster board and the roof of a timber frame construction. On the outside, the roof tiles are most likely to be made of concrete with felt underneath and, in many cases, some form of internal insulation. The foundations of these properties are typically of a concrete strip or a deeper pile foundation (see page 20). This means that they are solid in their construction and it is possible that a single storey extension would have foundations strong enough to take a second storey.

Some modern homes have even been built to allow for future improvements, such as loft conversions or two-storey extensions. If you have bought a new home within the last ten years, it is worth contacting the builder to ask any questions you may have about improvements you are planning, as this may save time and money spent on specialist help.

Flats

Since the late 1990s, there have also been some changes in the types of properties built, especially the number

For more information on foundations, see pages 20–1, and for a detailed look at roof structures – particularly in relation to extending up into a loft space – see pages 24–5 and 149–52.

of flats being created in city centres. In the main, blocks of flats are built in the same way as houses, just on a larger scale. As such, they are either brick and block walls or brick around timber frame construction. Many of the roof structures are either timber frame, just like a house, or are flat roofs that require regular maintenance.

Property improvement for flats is mostly restricted by your leasehold agreement and ensuring that any noise made is kept to a minimum. For new or renovated flat blocks, there is an increased specification required when building. Since 2003, for example, new rules and regulations regarding noise insulation for flooring require types of insulation that reduce the noise from the flat above. If you do live in a flat and are planning property improvements, make sure you check your leasehold agreement and with your freeholder before you undertake anything major.

FOUNDATIONS

There are two main types of foundations and which is the right type for your home depends on whether you are building a one- or two-storey extension and the stability of the land you are building on.

Strip foundation

This is a dug trench filled with concrete to a depth of 30cm or more and the bricks are then laid on top. These foundations are typically 1–1.5m deep and are usually constructed on stable, solid ground that is well compacted and able to take a building load. In some cases, where the land is stable but fairly soft (soft clay or a peaty soil, for example) or where far below the surface there are things such as mines or other underground passages, then a deeper foundation may be required.

Pile foundation

This is one of the most stable foundations. Deep foundations tend to be used for extra stability, when solid ground is in excess of 1m below the surface or where a particularly heavy load is being placed on the land or the land has had some underground excavation. These foundations usually go down at least 2m and can be up to 5m deep. Typically, the piles are made of steel or in some

66 There are two types of foundations, and this influences whether you are able to build a one- or two-storey extension. **99**

The legal aspects of developing your property are covered on pages 48-76, with specific information for flats and leasehold owners being discussed on pages 73-4.

cases concrete and they are secured with liquid concrete.

Latterly, to help improve the speed in which foundations can be built, concrete blocks are used instead of pouring concrete into the ground. This reduces the number of materials required and, of course, the drying time that the liquid concrete would take.

What this means is that you need to get professional help from a local expert when extending your home, trying to work out which foundations you have and whether they are good enough for the improvements you want to make. As a quick guide:

- **Properties built prior to the 1960s:** it is likely that the foundations will not be strong enough to build on further.

- **In the 1960s,** building regulations were revised with a new advisory committee, resulting in more detailed guidelines on the materials and methods that must be used when building.

However, every home is individual, so you can only rely on this information early on when thinking about what improvements you can make. Don't use this as a decision-making guide and take advice later before going too much further.

❝ You must get professional help from a local expert when deciding how to extend your home. ❞

The land your home is sitting on

When considering adding additional living accommodation, it is important to understand what type of land your property is sitting on as well as the strength of the foundations. Ideally, it would be built on stable, solid ground, which had nothing built underneath, such as a mine. However, in the UK, much land is sandstone, limestone, soft clay and even peat. Unfortunately, these materials are not especially stable, and issues such as the lack of rainfall in recent years have caused much of our clay to dry out, causing some subsidence in particular areas.

Bear in mind, too, that more rivers are flooding now and as we have become desperate to build more properties, building has been allowed on floodplains, which were previously seen as 'safe', but are now flooding regularly. In addition, we have contaminated some land in the UK with waste, which can be damaging if built on without using proper construction methods to protect you from poisonous gases such as methane. So before you start adding new space to the property, you will need to ensure the land is safe to build on and doesn't need any additional precautions.

WALLS

Wall structures are much easier than foundations to see and understand. Typically, there is an outside wall, which is naturally load bearing, some internal load-bearing walls and partition walls, which are used to create more rooms rather than support the structure.

In the main, outside walls are built of stone or brick and in some cases brick and block. Old properties can be fixed with a mix of mud, clay and straw, but later properties are likely to be joined together with mortar and some are integrated within a timber frame, while others are solid.

Stone walls

Depending on the type of stone, the outside wall is likely to be up to 60cm or more. Any property improvements will ideally use a similar type of stone, which might take time to source, will be more expensive than bricks and may well require the help of a stone mason. It will also take more work to knock or drill any holes and will need tough, professional equipment rather than the cheaper versions, which are only for light work.

Brick walls

Properties with brick outer walls will be 'double skin'. In walls built before the 1930s, they are likely to be solid, whereas those built since are likely to have a **cavity** between the two brick walls, at least on the ground floor – unless the property has a timber frame, which is an insulator in its own right. All homes built since 1995 should have been built with insulation already fitted.

Jargon buster

Attic trusses Special roof supports that lend themselves to creating a room in the roof

Cavity The space between a double skin wall

Double skin Two bricks that are laid side by side

Flashing Material, usually lead, that makes external joins waterproof, for example where a chimney meets the top of the roof

Hipped roof A standard roof that slopes up on all sides to a point

Lintel A beam, often made of stone, that is placed above a window or door opening to support the structure

Load bearing wall An essential wall that is integral to the structure of a home and, if taken away, will need to be supported

RSJ Rolled steel joist, added to a wall for strength

 For further information on what type of wall you have, the Energy Savings Trust have good descriptions to show the difference between a solid wall and one with a cavity – go to www.energysavingstrust.org.uk.

Partition walls

Internal partition walls are often thinner or even have a 'hollow' sound when you tap them. With brick- or stone-built properties, you can often see the thickness of a solid wall. In older properties, there may also be partition walls made of lathe and plaster with a timber joist frame. You can usually take these down, but be prepared for a horrendous mess as they are typically extremely dusty!

Since the 1930s, partition walls are typically made with wooden battens covered with board, which is sometimes insulated in between. These are easy to spot and easy to take down or move as they mostly sound hollow when you 'knock' along the wall.

Cracks in walls

All old homes and some new ones suffer from small cracks, but it is important to ensure they aren't serious before making any improvements. To find out, look at the survey you had done when you bought the property to see what it says about any cracks. If you haven't got a copy, ask the surveyor to send you another.

Most cracks appear either at the top of walls and around door or window frames. Small cracks that have been around for years and haven't changed in shape can just be filled in. The ones to watch out for are those that increase in length and widen over a period of time. These tend to be more serious and require a professional to help find out what is causing the problem.

 Structural problems, such as subsidence, that cause cracks usually appear 'overnight'. Severe cracks that appear on both the inside and out may suggest that the property is 'on the move'. Another clue is that doors and windows don't shut particularly well, especially when they did in the past. A well-known test is to get a 10p coin and see if it will fit in the crack. If any of your walls have a problem like this, it is well worth bringing in a surveyor to check having contacted your insurance company for advice.

Cracks in walls occur for several reasons, as follows:

- When a doorway or a window frame has not been strengthened above with a lintel or RSJ, which can cause the wall above to sag and cracks occur towards the corners. This is fairly simple to address by getting a professional to check whether there is a lintel/RSJ and if there isn't, it can be fixed by putting one in.
- If too much weight is laid to bear on the structure. For example, if a new roof or loft extension is fitted on a Victorian property without additional support. This may cause walls to bow

23

and cracks to form, and would need to be fixed quickly.

- **Settlement of a new property's weight on the land or plaster drying out.** Normally cracks that appear over time are fine and therefore can just be filled in. If this does happen and you are in a new property, contact the builder and they should fix it out for you via the NHBC building guarantee, which is a type of insurance that comes with all new homes and lasts for ten years. It typically covers the structure of the property and therefore allows you to make a claim if something like this goes wrong.

❝ Roof structures that best lend themselves to loft extensions have a large 'hipped' structure. These typically date from before the 1970s. ❞

ROOFS

Any roof is likely to be supported by a timber frame and its type and style depends on the age of the property and the region it was built in. Roof structures that best lend themselves to loft extensions are those with a large 'hipped' structure that you can easily stand up in. These are typically built before the 1970s. Properties built after the 1970s are usually difficult to convert as there is a criss-cross pattern of timber in the roof. Properties built more recently may have **attic trusses** to allow conversion at a later stage.

To check on your roof's condition (which is best done annually), go into the roof space without putting a light on and see if there are any gaps where light is coming in. Then turn on a light and check the beams for any damp patches. Many roof spaces are covered in a type of lining, which may be felt, and/or insulation between the beams, so make sure this is all secure.

At the same time, check the thickness of any insulation between the floor joists. This should be at least 15cm thick to prevent heat from being lost from the property.

Externally, most roof structures can be assessed by the naked eye. When checking your roof, look at the chimneys to see if they are straight and especially

 Turn to pages 149-52 for more information on extending your space up into the roof.

to see if there are any bulges or cracks where the chimney joins the roof structure. If the chimney is not used, make sure there is a 'cap' on top so that water cannot get in. Also ensure the bottom of the chimney stack is fully sealed with **flashing** and doesn't have any cracks in it.

Tiles

Tiles, whatever they are made of, should be completely fixed to the roof. Loose tiles can do huge amounts of damage to the roof's structure by letting in water or disappearing in windy conditions, exposing whole areas of your roof, which you'd have to pay through the nose to have fixed fast.

Guttering

Leaking guttering causes untold amounts of damage to a property and is easy and cheap to fix for most properties.

Check the guttering when it is raining and with binoculars, if necessary, to see if there are leaks in joints or if the guttering is full of rubbish and the water 'floods' over the top. Fix any problems immediately.

LISTED BUILDINGS

A listed building is one that has special preservation orders on it, which are decided by the relevant government department (see box, below). For most listed buildings, whether they are Grade 1 or 2, the following property improvements need to be passed by the local authority before you commence with any work.

Any changes to the external façade of the building, such as repairing or rebuilding chimneys, roof coverings, replacing windows and doors and any type of extension. It even means that you cannot take down any part of the

❝ You need to apply for permission before making any changes to the external façade of a listed building, as well as many internal features. ❞

Government building departments

England: English Heritage
Wales: CADW (Welsh Assembly Government's historic environment division)
Scotland: Historic Scotland
Northern Ireland: Department of the Environment

The websites for government building departments are: www.english-heritage.org.uk (English Heritage), www.cadw.wales.gov.uk (CADW), www.historic-scotland.gov.uk (Historic Scotland) and www.environ.ie (Department of the Environment).

property without their permission. In some cases, it may even stop you from being able to create a hard area on which to park your car or affect the type of fencing you have.

Many internal features are also covered, especially things such as fireplaces and fixtures, mouldings on ceilings, picture rails, dado rails or original tiles. So don't take any of these out without planning permission as it can put you in breach of the rules and regulations or, worse still, could reduce the value of your property.

Conservation areas, areas of natural beauty and National Parks

Restrictions here are varied and depend on the rules imposed locally. They can be similar to those of listed buildings or just apply to new properties being built or ones that people want to demolish. If you live in an area like this, seek help and advice from your local council. Be aware that it might not just be your property that is affected, but rules may even stretch to retaining specific trees within your garden.

Restricted controls on properties

Your local council will tell you if you are in a conservation area, an area of natural beauty or a National Park. To establish if your property is listed, check your original survey. The company that did your legal work should have made sure you were aware of owning a listed building. The bonus is that you may well be eligible for a grant to help towards the cost of the work (see pages 38-9).

If you are under restricted development, make sure you consult a local architect or surveyor and your council to ensure you know what you can and cannot do before you incur any costs. Be prepared that any planning permission requested may take longer than normal and that you may need to appeal to gain approval for the work. It may also take longer to secure the right people to work on your property due to the specialist nature of their job.

Money matters

When working on any home improvement project, two things will always happen to your budget. First, it is easy to forget the odd material required or job needed. For example, when fitting new carpets, you may have to pay for cutting the bottom off the doors so they can still open and shut. Second, halfway through, you find some different, more expensive items and this pushes up costs. The name of the game is to be as accurate as you can, then have a contingency for 'unexpected' costs.

2

How to budget

When improving a home, start planning your budget from the beginning. It is also important to make sure you have enough cash available, as you don't want to run out halfway through. If you need to borrow more money, you don't want to take out too much or too little, as this may cost you more in the long run.

In some cases, particularly for old or very individual properties, it will be difficult to know the final cost until the job is finished, so you need a high level of contingency in your budget. This is because problems may occur that were impossible to predict prior to starting the job. For example, when excavating for an extension, an old pipe might be found that needs to be identified and then taken out, or the electrics that looked like they would be easy to add to the existing wiring don't work, requiring more expense to identify and fix the problem.

Jargon buster

Contingency An amount of money over and above the budget to cover the cost of any unknown work

CREATING YOUR BUDGET

It is helpful to have a guide of everything you need to think about when creating your budget. If you have use of a computer, devising a spreadsheet can save time by showing what impact any changes or new quotes will have on your overall budget.

There are two ways to create your budget. The first is to create a budget by each room and the second is to create a budget per job, such as adding a conservatory or a loft extension, building a garage, painting or electrics. In the table given overleaf, there is a broad summary of the costs to consider for your project when starting to budget. Thereafter, in each chapter there are more bespoke lists for specific home improvement projects.

❝ A contingency sum is essential to cover unpredicted events. ❞

Planning a contingency sum

Type of project	Suggested contingency
Old property	30% of budget
Small jobs	10-15% of budget
Large jobs	20% of budget

FREE INFORMATION

There are certain pieces of free advice that you can get hold of, but be aware that free advice is only helpful at the planning stage. When you are going ahead with a project, it is better to pay for the advice you need so that the person giving the information is accurate and, better still, you may have some comeback should the advice turn out to be incorrect.

Help with planning permission

Some of the most valuable help that you can get free when considering a project that will need planning permission is advice from your local planning office. Be aware that they are likely to be very busy as they have to look after all the commercial and residential planning for the area. It is best if you contact them in plenty of time, say three months or more before you start your project. Write or call to make them aware of what it is you are hoping to do, and typically they will make a visit to the property. Sometimes they do this with you there, other times they will visit when you aren't around and send you a letter. If you can meet them, it will help as they could give you some initial advice on whether your application would be accepted or what you would need to do

to make sure the planning is approved on the first application (see pages 60–3).

Help with specific projects

All the trade associations that support the home improvement industry, such as the Federation of Master Builders, the Tile Association or the Basement Information Centre, supply free fact sheets, booklets and guidelines to help with your project. This can help when budget setting as it will give you an idea of everything you need to consider and the likely costs per day/hour that each profession charges (see Useful addresses, pages 210–13).

An amazing resource for all renovation projects are the numerous shows around the country that you can usually gain free entry to if you book early. Spend the day speaking to the different exhibitors, seeing and comparing different products and attending seminars on the types of things that you need to consider. There are usually some great deals on offer, but don't jump straight in and buy before you have researched the project thoroughly. Try asking a company whose products/ services you are interested in to hold the deal for you after the show or go back to another show to secure the offer at a later date once you've had time to consider the options.

Some websites for building shows and exhibitions are: www.granddesigns.co.uk, www.idealhomeshow.co.uk, www.thefurnitureshow.co.uk, www.bbcgoodhomesliveit.com, www.glassex.com and www.bkexpo.co.uk.

Items to consider for your budget

This table lists the key costings you need to consider and budget for, depending on your home improvement project. Although these lists are not exhaustive, they should cover most of the budgetary considerations you will need. Add any other items you think of under the 'Other' heading at the foot of the table.

Item	Budget (£s)	
Building works	Proposed	Actual
Labour		
Materials		
Equipment hire		
Preparation work (clearance/demolition)		
Windows		
Doors		
Damp-proofing		
Insulation		
Fireplaces		
Outbuildings		
Electrics		
Lighting		
Trunking		
Additional sockets		
New wiring		
Moving sockets/wiring		
Appliances		

Item	Budget (£s)	
	Proposed	Actual
Heating/plumbing		
Pipework		
Boiler		
Radiators		
Sink/bath/shower/toilet		
Thermostats		
Fireplaces		
Appliances		
Decoration		
Walls		
Floor		
Ceiling		
Accessories		
Furnishings		
Furniture		
Lamps		
Curtains		
Cushions		
Accessories		
Other		
TOTAL		

PAYMENT STAGES

When you are improving a property, there are usually different 'stages' involved. It is important to be aware of each of these and tie them in with when you pay for the work. This can save you money during the project and also means you have the cash needed to pay for the work. The four main stages for most projects are:

- Preparation
- First fix
- Second fix
- Finish.

Depending on your project, each of these stages could mean different things. For example, if you are planning an extension, preparation might mean taking down an old building or wall and preparing the groundwork for the foundations and walls to be built. First fix would be adding in the 'unseen' electrics and plumbing and second fix could be things like light switches on the now built walls and/or connecting up wiring/pipes to the mains. Finishing would be final decoration, such as painting.

At each stage of this work, you may have to pay some money upfront, such as a fixed amount, say around £250–£500 or a percentage of the cost of the work, for example 5–10 per cent. It is essential to never pay the full amount upfront. If you do, the builder/contractor could disappear with your cash or the items delivered could be faulty. Most companies and tradespersons are happy to be paid in stages or even when a job is completed to your satisfaction.

Planning your payments is important if you are borrowing money or drawing down from savings. For example, if the total project is £30,000, you may only need £5,000 for materials at the start of the work, £10,000 after six weeks work, £10,000 twelve weeks later with the final £5,000 paid once the work is completed. Keeping your money in a savings account or not paying the interest on the borrowed amount could save you hundreds of pounds to put towards those extras at a later date. To help give you a guideline of the types of costs for different projects, see the table opposite.

In addition, get guidance for local costs by speaking to friends, family and neighbours. Visit their property improvement and find out what it cost, how long it took and what help they could give you with contacts or even pointers of things they would do differently next time around.

You can also get bespoke quotes and ask the tradesperson or company why they may be significantly different from the information provided in the guideline costs and get a second and third opinion to be sure you are being quoted fairly.

Home improvement costs

Home improvement costs are notoriously difficult to predict or estimate. The figures opposite are purely for guidance as every home is different and anyone that improves their home will want to do so in a different way.

Examples of home improvement costs

	Guide price (per square metre)	Budget/easy	Premium/bespoke
Building			
One-storey extension	£550–£1,250	£7,000	£35,000
Two-storey extension	£800–£2,000	£15,000	£50,000
Garage	Self-build: £20–£50	£1,000	£8,000
	Built: £200–£500	£5,000	£40,000
Conservatory	£225–£3,000	£6,000	£35,000
Basement	£1,000–£2,500	£40,000	£100,000
Conversion			
Loft	£750–£2,000	£18,000	£50,000
Garage	£400–£1,000	£9,000	£25,000
Basement	£500–£2,500	£10,000	£50,000
Additions			
Swimming pool	£100–£1,250	£10,000	£70,000
Garden building (summer house/office)	£70–£250	£1,000	£20,000
Driveway	£45–£90	£1,000	£8,000
External work			
Roofing	£45–£100	–-	–-
Windows	£350–£1,000 each*	–-	–-
External doors	£100–£500 each*	–-	–-
Internal work			
Internal doors	£30–£300 each*	–-	–-
Boiler	£400–£1,200 each	–-	–-
Radiators	£50–£500 each	–-	–-
Wiring	N/A	£2,000	£7,000

* Sum includes furniture and fitting

Budget/Easy: This is the minimum price for a home improvement, where labour rates for the work are low. The improvement would be small scale and only require standard building practices and materials. For example, a one-storey extension 3 x 1m built on standard foundations using cheapest brick or brick/block, which is easy to join to the current roof structure.

Premium/Bespoke: These prices are for areas that have high labour rates and for large-scale improvements or where additional work is required. For example, a 3 x 3m extension in a conservation area that requires more expensive materials to be used or additional work, such as moving drains or the extension requiring specialist foundations.

PLANNING TIME

Trying to estimate the time it takes to do any job on a property is difficult without a specific quote as each property is different. For example, decorating a 5 x 5m room might only require an undercoat of paint, then one topcoat, which could be done in a day. Alternatively, it might be that the walls need to be sanded down to remove previous paint, then cracks filled, two undercoats applied followed by three colour coats of paint, which could take a full week.

The table opposite gives timeframes for how long a project might take from planning to completion on an average three-bedroom detached home. This is only a guideline as every project is different, so you will need to confirm these timings with your local authority, if you are seeking planning and building regulations approval, together with your contractors.

BUYING MATERIALS

When carrying out a home improvement project, you have a choice of buying from:

- **The supplier direct,** e.g. Johnstones Paint or Furness Bricks
- **A builders' merchant,** e.g. Jewson or Build Centre
- **DIY retail outfit,** e.g. B&Q or Brewers

❝Every project is different and timescales vary. Confirm the timings relating to planning and building regulations with your local authority.❞

Throughout the book there are different projects included. On page 202 there is a chart similar to the one opposite that outlines approximate lengths of time for the most popular jobs.

Planning your time

Project	Planning	Lead time from order to delivery**	Average time to carry out project
Extensions*			
Two-storey	24 weeks	3 months–1 year	12 weeks
One-storey	16 weeks	3 months–1 year	6 weeks
Garage	16 weeks	3 months–1 year	3 weeks
Conservatory	12 weeks	6 weeks	1–2 weeks
Basement	12 weeks	6 weeks	2–4 weeks
Conversions*			
Loft	16 weeks	12 weeks	2–8 weeks
Garage	10 weeks	2 weeks	2–4 weeks
Basement	16 weeks	4 weeks	1 week
Additions			
Swimming pool	16 weeks	4 weeks	2 weeks
Garden landscaping	12 weeks	4 weeks	1–2 weeks
Garden building	4 weeks	4 weeks	1–10 days
Kitchen	4 weeks	0–6 weeks	3–10 days
Bathroom	4 weeks	0–6 weeks	3–10 days
Security system	2 weeks	2 weeks	1–2 days
Home automation system	2 weeks	2 weeks	2 weeks+
Replacements			
Windows	6 weeks	2–6 weeks	1–2 days
Doors	1 week	0–2 weeks	1–2 days
Wiring	2 weeks	N/A	2–3 days
Central heating system	2 weeks	1 week	1–2 days

* Assumes planning permission/regulations required. If these are not necessary, planning time can be halved

** Includes time to book professional help and materials

- Online, e.g. www.Screwfix.net
- OR you can ask your builder, electrician or other professional to purchase on your behalf.

If you are getting a quote from a professional, ask for the materials and labour charges to be quoted separately

Property tips

- Large food retailers have an aisle for DIY items, so it is worth checking them out as well as DIY stores as they tend to be competitively priced. The downside is that you don't get as much choice.
- Before going to a builder's merchant or similar, make sure you have a detailed list of everything you need, including sizes and dimensions.
- Whatever price you are given, ask for at least 10 per cent discount or, better still, ask what discount they can give and try to get more money off, particularly for large projects. Always check these against the price of a local specialist, such as local electrical wholesaler or timber merchant and what your tradesman/builder is quoting.

so that you can see if the tradesperson or company is charging you a premium for ordering the products. If you are ordering from one of the DIY retailers, don't forget they are likely to charge a fee for delivery if you are over a certain mile radius, whereas if you are ordering from a builders' merchant, they will tend to deliver for free as the items are much bigger and are bought in bulk.

Both online and high street retailers tend to be competitive on 'headline' items that they promote, such as plasterboard or a drill, but then vary dramatically on all other products, so it is worth shopping around before you buy.

As a basic guide, it is worth visiting a builders' merchant if:

- Your project involves major building materials, such as bricks, cement, sand and wood.
- It is a large building project, such as a one- or two-storey extension.
- You are upgrading your kitchen or bathroom.
- You are buying a new conservatory.
- They have specialist in-store equipment hire.
- You are landscaping your garden, especially if you are planning on using stone, gravel or fencing.

 For more information on getting quotes from contractors, see pages 79 and 96–7.

Compare prices

Once you have information from your builder/tradesman and prices from a merchant, direct from a supplier or the DIY retailers, compare the price quotes. Don't forget to include in this comparison any guarantees for materials or labour and delivery charges as these may make the difference between which quote you accept.

Make sure you visit the right merchant branch by calling them first. Not all merchant branches stock everything they sell, so if you want to look at kitchens or hire equipment, you need to make sure they have everything you need before you visit. Also, some branches like dealing with the general public, while others prefer to deal with the trade only, so ask them before you visit if they are happy to help you.

❝ Online and high street retailers are competitive on 'headline' items, but other prices vary dramatically. ❞

Funding your development

There are lots of different ways of financing your home improvement. Unfortunately, unlike mortgages or some loans secured on your property, loans in general are not regulated and there is no 'standard' way of selling finance to enable you to compare different finance packages easily so choose your funding carefully.

It isn't possible to suggest how best to fund your home improvement as that depends on your financial circumstances and should always get advice from an independent financial adviser. However, we can suggest how to check if there are grants available towards the costs of your repairs or improvements. If you don't qualify for a grant, then there are four main options (which you can mix and match) to choose from to fund your home improvement costs.

UTILISING CURRENT SAVINGS

In theory, this is the cheapest and most straightforward way of funding your home improvement. However if this is the only money that you have, it is worth finding a back-up source of funding, should your project go over budget.

The benefits of using your savings are that you can ensure that you have the money to hand and, if this is a 'finite' resource, you may work harder to ensure the project comes in on budget. If you are using your savings, it is important to draw down the money only when required so that you can maximise the interest you earn on your savings.

HOME IMPROVEMENT GRANTS

Grants for home improvements are typically for essential repairs and many are means tested to ensure you cannot afford them in the first place. Apart from help towards energy saving in the home, most grants are gained via your local council or a home improvement agency. Each council runs grants differently, so it is worth investigating what is and isn't available as soon as you decide you are going ahead with your project. This is especially relevant if you are over 60 or disabled or live in a listed or substandard property.

For information on independent financial advisers, go to the Financial Services Authority website at www.fsa.gov.uk.

Home improvement grants

Type of grant	Detail	Where to find out more
Energy saving	Discounts off loft and cavity wall insulation; discounts off energy efficient appliances; grants towards a new boiler and low carbon products.	www.energysavingstrust.org.uk www.lowcarbonbuildings.org.uk
Listed buildings	For major works, such as structural repair.	Your local authority and/or regional office of English Heritage: www.English-heritage.org.uk
Renovation grants	These are rarely available for someone who owns their own home/is a landlord. They are usually available to bring a property back to liveable, safe conditions. They are also likely to be means tested.	For England and Wales: http://local.direct.gov.uk For Scotland: www.Scotland.gov.uk For Northern Ireland: www.nihe.gov.uk
Disability grants	Available for those that need to adapt their property to enable them to remain in their home. Means tested, but can help buy products to help you move around the property, such as a stair lift, or to widen doors.	www.direct.gov.uk
Other grants for those in need and the elderly	Available for essential repairs.	www.foundations.uk.com

 More help for home improvements relating to the disabled is given on pages 171-7.

INCREASING YOUR MORTGAGE

This is a popular way of funding large improvement projects that will usually add extra space and ideally increase the value of your property, making it worth paying off over a longer period of time. It is often referred to as 'secured lending' as the money is borrowed against your home, meaning that the lender has more chance of getting their money back if you cannot pay.

The main benefits of funding your home improvement via this method are that you can spread the payment over the term of your loan – so if you have 20 years left to pay of your mortgage, you can have 20 years to pay off the cost. It is also likely that if you have ensured you are switching your mortgage regularly to get the best deal, then the

interest rate should be lower than a personal loan.

When considering this option, you need to be aware just how much borrowing via your mortgage will cost you over the period of the loan. Don't forget that if interest rates go up during the time you are paying it back, you may end up paying back more money over time, whereas on a loan, the interest rate is usually fixed until you pay it off (see pages 43–4).

It is also likely to take time to get the approval for lending via your mortgage, which could range from the same day to up to eight weeks for large amounts. It may involve the cost of someone doing a valuation of the property and is therefore something that you need to plan ahead for when spending on your home improvement project.

Funding your home: a ready reckoner

The following figures are the incremental cost of increasing your mortgage from £130,000 to £160,000, based on a repayment mortgage, not interest only. They don't take into account the cost of organising the increased mortgage, which depends on the type of mortgage and your lender. If you have a flexible mortgage or 'one' account, you may not incur any charges for increasing the mortgage unless a revised valuation of the property is required.

Length of time for borrowing the money	5%	6%	7%	8%
10-year term	38,400	40,560	42,600	45,000
15-year term	44,100	45,900	49,500	52,200
20-year term	48,000	52,800	57,600	60,480
25-year term	53,400	58,500	64,500	70,500

If you were borrowing £30,000 to add a conservatory to your property, the table opposite guides you through the likely costs. Bear in mind that you may incur an 'administration' charge for increasing your mortgage, which could be up to £600.

To find out if you can increase your mortgage to fund your home improvement:

- **Contact or book a meeting with your mortgage lender** and ask them to explain their process and timings.
- **Most lenders will offer to increase the loan**, as long as you maintain some equity in your home. This range varies according to the lender and some have a limit. For example, they may not let you borrow more than 85 or 95 per cent of the value of the home.
- **Ask whether you have to borrow over the full term** of the mortgage, or if you can borrow over a shorter term and ask for the final cost (as in the table opposite).
- **Find out if there are any fees** to increase your mortgage, charges vary from a hundred pounds upwards.

❝ Check your mortgage interest rate now. ❞

SWITCHING YOUR MORTGAGE

If you are thinking of taking out more money via your mortgage to fund your home improvement, this might be a good time to check that you are on the very best rate. The table opposite shows that a slight change in the percentage interest rate that you pay, or the length of time you pay off the mortgage can make a substantial difference to what you pay back.

For example, if you are currently paying 7 per cent interest rate for your mortgage, but by re-mortgaging to increase your loan from £100,000 to £130,000, a lower interest rate of, say, 5 per cent could actually save you nearly £10,000 over a 20-year loan period. On a monthly basis, this would mean your monthly payments, based on a repayment mortgage, would be £870 instead of £1,025. However, these savings need to be balanced against any costs you may incur by paying off your current mortgage early. Many lenders have moved away from charges for paying off your mortgage early after much campaigning by the press, but check with your lender as redemption penalties can run into several thousands of pounds.

Re-mortgaging takes time and often requires you to pay money upfront to

Search websites such as www.switchwithwhich.co.uk and www.moneysupermarket. co.uk to find the best deal, including all the costs involved, and contact an independent financial adviser (IFA) via www.unbiased.co.uk to ensure you have the right mortgage for your long-term needs.

switch to another lender. It is worth shopping around for the best deal over the term of the mortgage and not just signing up to a great deal on a short-term basis (see box, page 41).

When re-mortgaging, the process is more complicated as the new lender needs to have a legal agreement between you and them, so that if you don't make the agreed payments they can repossess the property. Most lenders will do this within two to four weeks, but some can take longer. Ensure you know when the money is going to be available before committing to your expenditure. The order of events to re-mortgage is as follows:

Step 1 Research and compare your current mortgage deal to new ones via the internet and an IFA (see box, page 41).

Step 2 Fill in the lender's application form and sign. You may have to provide a proof of income via wage slips or a letter from your employer/accountant.

Step 3 The lender will value your home by sending one of their trained staff or a qualified surveyor.

Step 4 The lender may offer 'free conveyancing' for the legal work or you will have to appoint a company yourself. They will contact your existing lender for a statement of the final amount of money you owe.

Step 5 If the valuation confirms that the property is worth the money (with the extra improvements), then a final offer

will be made by the new lender, including the new monthly payments you will need to make.

Step 6 The new mortgage is confirmed and any additional monies that you borrow will be paid once the legal company has deducted its fees (unless this was paid for by the lender).

❝ If you take out a secured loan – a second mortgage – it is important to know that failure to keep repaying the mortgage can result in your home being repossessed. ❞

In some cases, if you increase your mortgage as a percentage of the value (for example, move from a mortgage that is 85 per cent of the value of the property to 95 per cent), you may also require a mortgage indemnity premium, which can cost several thousand pounds. Make sure that you check this with the lender/IFA before you agree to re-mortgage.

TAKING OUT A LOAN

There are two types of loan that you can take out to cover your home improvement costs. What kind you choose depends on:

- The amount you need to borrow.
- Whether you own a home or not.
- Your personal financial circumstances, such as bad credit or being self-employed.

Secured loan

This is usually the cheapest way to secure a loan and it is where you agree to place a 'second' charge on your property so that if you cannot repay the loan for any reason, the lender can recoup the monies owed by insisting your property is sold.

The minimum secured loan is usually £3,000 to £75,000 and is taken out from three to 25 years. Unlike when increasing your mortgage, loans can be made up to 125 per cent of the value of your home, including the mortgage that you owe, so if you do not have enough equity in your home to increase you mortgage to fund your home improvements, a secured loan may be the next best option.

Other advantages of a secured loan are that if you are self-employed or have had problems with bad debts or county court judgements, then securing a loan against your property is easier than trying to take out a personal loan. The rates are usually cheaper, so you should end up paying back less money for the loan and, unlike increasing your mortgage, there are rarely any costs such as legal, valuation or redemption costs associated with the loan.

Unsecured loan

Unsecured lending is taking out a loan with no guarantee to the lender that you are going to pay back the money. This doesn't mean they won't pursue you vigorously should you not pay. Unsecured loans are usually for smaller projects and range from £500 to £25,000. The payback time ranges from six months to ten or more years.

The differences between unsecured lending over secured lending or increasing your mortgage are:

- **You do not put your home at risk** should you not be able to pay back the loan (although the lender will chase you for the money is some way, shape or form).
- **The process is much quicker** and can usually be done within days rather than weeks.

However, the downside is that the cost of the loan – the interest rate charged –

43

Jargon buster

APR Annualised percentage rate
IFA Independent financial adviser
PPI Payment protection insurance

If you are taking out a loan, make sure that you are aware of exactly how much you will be paying back and if the rate charged is fixed or variable.

Also check if there are any penalties or monies you need to pay back if you pay off the loan early.

can be more than you would pay if increasing your mortgage or borrowing with a secured loan.

Unlike mortgages, secured and unsecured loans are not regulated by the FSA, but they are subject to the Consumer Credit Act of 1974. This was introduced to help consumers compare loans. One thing that you must be aware of for comparison purposes is the annualised percentage rate (APR). This already applies to credit cards and anyone loaning money must, by law, calculate and make clear the APR, including within it any fees they may charge to set up the loan.

Protection insurance

Some companies add 'protection insurance' to any loans you consider. This is an insurance charge that covers part or all of your payments should you not be able to pay. It can be a good thing if it is charged at a reasonable rate and you are not penalised if you pay off your loan early. However, it can run into thousands of pounds, so make sure you ask if the quote includes protection insurance and what its terms are.

COMPANY FINANCING OPTIONS

There are many home improvement companies that now offer credit facilities for you to purchase your home improvement, be it a kitchen, conservatory or even building work. These schemes can be more expensive than purchasing finance directly from a finance company who compete in the whole loan market, rather than just in one area.

Finance is offered in two different ways. They either have their own 'branded' financial service business, such as Marks and Spencer or MFI, and although this may be provided by an existing finance company such as HSBC or HBOS, they are still a financial services company in their own right. Other companies offer finance options by 'referring' you to another finance company, where they may get a commission or an introducer's fee for doing so.

There are a variety of finance options that can be offered. Never agree to go with any of these deals until you are sure that it is the best way of funding your home improvement project. Here is a guide to the different types of options you are likely to be offered.

Secured or unsecured loans

With loans such as these you must use an independent source to compare the total repayment costs against what you would make. You may well be offered an increased 'discount' if you take out a loan, to pay for the payment protection insurance (PPI). These discounts could be substantial – thousands of pounds – but without knowing what the final total of the money repaid will be, you may end up paying thousands more than you saved over time via the finance package. Always make sure there are no penalty payments to be made if you want to pay off the loan early. Some companies also try to persuade you to buy their

payment protection insurance (see box, opposite below).

Never sign up to this until you have checked out how much it would cost you via an independent company. According to one independent PPI provider called Payment Care, buying via the company that gives you the loan can cost five times as much as organising it independently. On a £10,000 loan, this can mean paying back as much as an extra £3,000.

Buy now, pay later

These are deals that are regularly offered, particularly on kitchens, bathrooms and soft furnishings. Normally you have to pay a deposit, which can start at £500. After you have given a deposit, these deals normally work in two ways. It may be that the offer is 'Buy now, pay in 12 months' and that after 12 months, you need to pay the full amount or you might only start paying monthly payments for the item six or 12 months later.

A deal whereby you don't have to pay anything for a period of time and then pay the full amount, which doesn't attract an increase in the amount you will have to pay, can be a good deal – as long as they are not inflating the price of the item for the privilege. However, if it is just a payment 'holiday' and you then start paying off the item, it may attract a higher interest rate charge, in which case, as with any loan, make sure you know what the total amount you have to repay will be and then you can compare this with other methods of borrowing money.

Home improvement companies can try to get you to sign on the dotted line for their home improvement finance package by offering you a discount if you fund it through them. Before signing anything, check the amount you will end up repaying – the loan APRs can vary dramatically.

Interest-free option

Some companies are so keen to sell you their products they will allow you to have the goods and sign up to a finance package that will require you to pay back the monies at an agreed monthly fee for a set period of time. There are lots of different ways that a company might offer this facility using, for example, a 'card' or via a credit agreement. The time offered ranges from days to weeks, months and even a year or two.

As long as any options you see like this don't include horrendous charges for payment protection insurance and the products aren't charged at an inflated rate, they are worth considering – but make sure you read all the small print first. Watch out for charges that may occur if you don't pay back all the money in time, as this may again negate the financial benefit of the interest-free payment period.

Borrowing on credit cards or via an overdraft

Unless you can borrow at zero per cent or a very low rate, then these are an expensive way to fund home improvements. Some banks offer free overdrafts and certainly, if you have been a customer for a long time, your bank may give you a good deal. However, they are more likely to want to sell you a loan.

With regard to credit cards, this is one of the most expensive ways of borrowing money unless you can get a zero per cent deal, which you don't have to pay back for six months or a year. Interest rates (APRs) charged by these companies can be in excess of 15 per cent of the annual interest rate.

❝Check the prices of interest-free products. ❞

The top five things you should consider when looking for finance

1 Talk to an independent financial adviser to work out what is the best way to finance your project.

2 Compare financing packages by looking at the total cost of the loan over the period you are borrowing for, rather than just the monthly payments.

3 Check the terms and conditions and small print of any financing deal – what happens if you want to pay a loan off early?

4 If you want to have protection insurance on a loan or other form of financing, make sure you search the market for the best value insurance. Check you are not tied in to using the lender's insurance policy, which may be much higher.

5 Before you spend the money on your home, make sure you check whether it will add real value to it.

Rules and regulations

What you can and cannot do in your own home alters day by day. The government is introducing long-term legal changes aiming to make properties easier to buy and safer to live in. Although the intentions are good, there are so many changes coming into force that even the professionals are struggling to keep up with new training, testing and legal requirements. This chapter guides you through the key elements.

Can you do it yourself?

We all have great intentions when starting DIY projects, but research tells us that four out of ten people don't finish jobs they start and we each spend approximately £1,700 putting right failed DIY jobs. The DIY jobs that you can do really depend on your ability, your experience, the time you have available and, more importantly, whether you are legally allowed to carry out certain jobs in your home (see page 51).

To do a DIY job you need to be able to assess the work that needs doing. For example, putting up a curtain pole sounds easy, but do you know how the wall is constructed and therefore the type of fixings that you need or even the types of drill bit and length required? Do you have a spirit level long enough to ensure the curtain pole is put up straight? Will the fixings be strong enough to hold heavy curtains? If you are laying laminate flooring, how good are you at maths so you can ensure you cut suitable angles to go around a doorframe.

It also requires knowledge of the types of tools needed – and the ability to use them! It's no use buying a cheap tile cutter if you are laying 2.5cm-thick floor tiles, or a basic sander or electric drill if you are carrying out major renovations on a home. If you've not done any DIY before, practise first. Go on a course (often local colleges run them) or practise on something that is acceptable to ruin. Don't do it on your own home or it could cost you thousands to have it put right!

If, on the other hand, you have experience of one trade, it is likely you can more easily adapt to another. A good bricklayer would probably find it relatively easy to tile or do carpentry work as the skills are similar, and vice versa. Whatever your level of experience, if you haven't done a job before, ask someone to give you a hand, maybe to start off the job, or to do the bits that you find difficult.

 It is important to be aware of health and safety measures when doing any DIY. It sounds alarming, but one person dies every week from falling off a ladder. Make sure you use all relevant safety equipment, such as goggles, dust masks and/or gloves, so that your keenness for DIY doesn't turn into a disaster that affects your health.

The type of finish you are looking for is another factor to consider. If the job is one that will make the property look fantastic, such as tiling in a bathroom or putting in a kitchen, it is probably better to pay a professional. However, if it is putting units into a utility room that few people will see or laying flooring in a loft space for storage purposes, then as long as you measure well, use the right tools (and keep to the roof timbers), then it's worth considering doing these yourself.

PLANNING TIME

One thing that holds most people up during DIY work is lack of time. We all think jobs can be done in a day or weekend, but what if you can't get it done in that time? What is your contingency plan? Jobs that take one weekend and need to be finished by Monday morning or for visitors the next week should be done with a spare weekend or few days' holiday, just in case. You don't want to let the relatives sleep in a half-finished room full of dust that hasn't yet settled, or that has an overpowering smell of paint. So however long you think it will take you, add some contingency time on a just-in-case basis.

TERRACED AND PARTLY ATTACHED PROPERTIES

If DIY goes wrong in a detached house, it is usually only your own property that is affected. However, if you live in a flat, it is likely to be leasehold and even putting up shelving could impact on the next-door property when walls are adjoining. If you are in a terrace, or partly attached property, although you are likely to own the freehold, work done on the property will need to be legal under the Party Wall Act (see page 52). If you are going to make any changes to shared walls (internal and external), floors and ceilings, driveways or other communal spaces/materials, then you need to gain written approval – and sometimes even planning permission (see pages 57–9).

Home Information Packs

With the introduction of Home Information Packs (HIPs) in the summer of 2007, think through what types of materials you use as this will lead to a better 'efficiency rating' for your home. Some are now legally required, such as gas boilers fitted in both new and existing homes (in England and Wales) must be, in the main, condensing boilers. They have to achieve an 'A' or 'B' efficiency rating and you (or the company that fits them) need to advise the local council it has been fitted as it forms part of the building regulations (see page 71).

 For more information on home information packs, see the *Which? Essential Guide Buy, Sell and Move House.*

How to assess what you can/cannot do

This table gives an idea of how easy or difficult the main home improvements jobs are to do.

Job examples	Rating
Beginners DIY	
Painting	1
Wallpapering	2
Putting up shelves/curtain poles/blinds	2
Replacing doors	2
Fitting locks	2
Garden landscaping	2
Installing basic security/equipment	1
Experienced DIY	
Changing lights	3
New ceilings/walls	4
Adding a new socket to existing circuit	4
Replacing/building a conservatory	4
Replacing existing plumbing	3
Laying flooring	3
Tiling	3
Erecting shed/kit garden building (no utilities)	2
Highly skilled DIY	
Plastering	5
Putting in new bathroom/kitchen	5
Replacing/fitting new windows	5
Property extension	5
Fitting solar panels/wind turbines	5
Building from new, e.g. garage	5
Electrical and gas work	5

Ratings scale explanation

1 Straightforward

2 Straightforward, depending on property fabric/ material

3 Requires some experience

4 Requires some specific training

5 Professional work only recommended

Summary of legal do's and dont's

These are the main legal requirements. At the moment, legislation mainly relates to gas, electricity and the water mains, but the government is consulting on whether further restrictions should apply to plumbing work too. There may be more and they need to be noted in conjunction with the planning/building regulations. If in doubt, ask a qualified professional.

Utility	Can't do	Can do	Advice
Gas	• Connect any gas appliance or pipe • Move existing pipes • Tamper with gas meter	• Lay a pipe from A to B • Turn gas on and off	www.trustcorgi.com
Electricity	• Complete rewiring • Wire to a fuse box, e.g. new circuit • Add new electrics, e.g. light, shower, cooker, socket outlet • Replace damaged electric cables • Add any new outdoor electricity connections • Tamper with electric meter	• Add an additional socket to existing circuit • Replace an existing light/other appliance • Change a plug/lightbulb/fuse • Add a breaker unit • Turn electricity on/off • Turn a fuse switch to 'on' if cut out • Turn a fuse switch to 'off' if replacing an appliance	www.niceic.org.uk
Water/Waste	• Connect to anyone else's water/drainage system (without formal agreement) • Connect or interfere with pipes/drainage outside your property's boundaries • Tamper with water meter	• Make a new connection to water mains on your property • Put in a shower, bath, sink • Connect pipes to water supply within the home • Change taps • Create/replace new waste pipes • Unblock pipes • Turn water on/off	Local water authority
Asbestos	• Dispose of asbestos as normal waste, only where 'hazardous waste' is accepted • Sand, drill or saw asbestos • Remove asbestos lagging, spray coatings or insulation board within a property	• Remove 'non-licenced' asbestos products, e.g. when in Artex or cement	Local council

 For further information on what you can and can't do legally, go to www.trustcorgi.com (gas), www.niceic.org.uk (electricity), www.water.org.uk or your local water board (water) and your local council for matters relating to asbestos.

PARTY WALLS

The Party Wall Act 1996 allows you to work on joint walls, such as putting up shelves, plastering and rewiring, without permission, as long as you only go to half of the width of the wall/ceiling/floor. However, any likely noise should be cleared with affected neighbours or they may make a formal complaint under the noise laws.

To work on joint walls, you need to give notice of the work you are going to do, then gain permission if you want to make any major changes to a party wall. For example, you need to notify neighbours if you want to increase the height or thickness of a joint wall to build an extension or convert an area or if you want to add/replace flashing that affects roof joins. This is also applicable if you are wanting to underpin a party wall, make it load bearing (apply an RSJ), and especially if you intend to do anything that could affect the neighbour's foundations. You don't want to be responsible for their property subsiding or falling down as a result of your home improvements!

To ensure you stay legal:

- **Write to the affected neighbour** (or owner of the property such as a landlord) a minimum of two months before work starts, and have proof, such as recorded delivery or an independent witness, that you have served notice. Note the day you delivered the letter.
- **If you have a flat,** you also need to check your lease for what work you can carry out and then write to the freeholder for advice/permission to carry out the work you want to do (see also pages 73–4).
- **Make sure you gain a written response** within 14 days; don't rely on a verbal agreement.
- **Don't carry out work** if they haven't bothered to respond – this just puts it in dispute.

If there is a dispute, a surveyor can be appointed (jointly or separately) and he or she will award a 'yes' or 'no' to the work you want to carry out. If you get a no, you have 14 days to appeal to a County Court, at which point you may want to double-check that this is the right type of home improvement to make. Even if you get a yes, unhappy neighbours can make jobs that affect their property very difficult to carry out, so try to get it all agreed first.

❝ Flat owners need the freeholder's permission for building work. ❞

 For more information about party walls, visit www.collier-stevens.co.uk.

Planning permission

The planning system has evolved in the UK since the mid nineteenth century. Its aim is to protect the environment we live in, be it the countryside, town or city.

In England and Wales (see pages 75–6 for Scotland and Northern Ireland) the system is described as being 'planning-led' and is enforced by the Planning and Compulsory Purchase Act 2004. There are more changes in the pipeline, which may ease the planning process for residential home improvements (see page 64).

For many, the planning system is extremely confusing and rarely appears consistent. In some cases, someone can request, and then have denied, extending a property sympathetically to its environment. A few months later, someone else can apply to build a new property only 200m away that isn't sympathetic, have it rejected, appeal and then have it approved.

There are two main reasons for this apparent lack of consistency:

- Each local authority creates its own rules – around their published Local Development Framework. It is this that often governs what happens in each area and why it may appear easier to gain planning permission in some areas than in others, particularly if they have been selected for regeneration or development in some way.

- Apart from permitted development, planning decisions are based to some extent on the 'rules', but these can be interpreted differently depending on who is making the decision. For example, if you have a planning department sympathetic to new construction methods and the latest architectural design, they may be more likely to pass modern home improvements than a department that is keen on a more traditional look.

When considering any major home improvements that are going to require planning permission, read your council's Local Development Framework where there may be a section on residential home improvements, such as 'extension of dwellings'. The framework can be incredibly helpful, giving a picture of what would and would not be acceptable.

“The council's Local Development Framework should guide you as to what development might be acceptable, as well as what would not.”

Jargon buster

Full planning permission Approval from your local authority for you to go ahead with the property improvements as indicated in the plans you have submitted to them

Outline planning permission An 'approval' in principle from the local authority, given subject to gaining full planning permission

Planning officer A person in the local authority who advises on changes to your property and how they might impact on nearby buildings, people and the environment

❝The Planning Portal lists permitted developments.❞

Even if your home improvement doesn't require planning permission, you may well require building regulation checks and a certificate. Make sure that you read the buildings regulation section (see pages 66–72) and consult your local building regulation control department if you are unsure. Check your plans with the planning department at your local authority (you can usually do this free before submitting).

WORK YOU CAN DO WITHOUT PLANNING PERMISSION

Improvements that can be made to a property without planning permission are called 'permitted development'. They only change if you have a particular type of property (such as a listed property) or you are in a specially designated area (such as a conservation area – see page 26). The Planning Portal has been created by the government to help you work out what developments are permitted.

Household extensions (not applicable to flats)

You can extend a house by less than 70cu m or increase its original volume by less than 15 per cent (to a maximum of 115cu m) without obtaining planning permission. If you have a terraced house, it's slightly less – under 50cu m or a 10 per cent increase in size.

This sounds simple, but what you need to remember is the word 'original' house. If someone has already increased the property size since 1948 (when these rules came in for the first time), you may not be able to add more space without applying for planning permission.

For single-storey extensions, the pitch of the roof cannot be more than 4m to the ridge or 3m for a flat roof. For two-storey extensions, you can build up to

 For more information on the Planning Portal, go to www.planningportal.gov.uk.

the current level of the roof. In some cases, this means that you can add a second storey above a garage, for example, without needing planning permission. To do this though, the extension needs to remain within 2m of the property's boundary.

Porches are usually allowed as long as they are not more than 3sq m externally in size, less than 3m high, or when built would be more than 2m away from the property's boundary and road/public footpath.

Buildings in the garden

In the main, garden buildings, such as sheds or swimming pools, don't need planning permission. However, they must not be for residential use and shouldn't front onto a road. The height needs to be restricted to 4m for a pitched and 3m for a flat roof – but kits rarely create them higher than this anyway. Also, you need to retain some of the garden for free space, so don't build anything that is more than half the size of the garden.

Adding a garage/off-road parking

Off-road parking is permitted as long as it is only on your land. No new route must be required to gain access to your garden either. Bear in mind that the space may only be used for private car ownership, not to park a fleet of company vans on it, and you will need to gain written approval from the highways department of your local council to drop the kerb from the road.

Converting a loft, garage or outbuilding

Loft conversions are permitted improvements as long as the overall dimensions of the property don't change. The conversion cannot increase the living space by more than 40cu m for a terraced property or 50cu m for a detached house and the roof height must be maintained.

Converting a garage or outbuilding always requires planning permission, unless the building is deemed as necessary for parking in areas where there is a shortage (London, for example). In these instances, whether planning permission is granted or not depends on how you intend to change its use. A call to your local planning office or visiting their website should give you an idea as to whether you need to apply for planning permission or not.

Windows and doors

New and replacement windows and doors only need permission in England and Wales if you are in a specially designated area. Even roof lights and skylights are fine and although they need to adhere to building regulations you don't need planning permission.

Walls, fences and gates

You are allowed to erect fences and walls (including hedges) if the height is less than 1m near the boundary to a public highway, or 2m elsewhere and there are no rules within your title deed about erecting fences (some have an 'open-plan' estate policy). However, as most

55

boundary markings will have some impact on a public highway, it is advisable to check with the planning office before you proceed.

Solar panels and wind turbines

The government is committed to encouraging people to make their homes more energy efficient. As a result, they are keen to make adding solar panels, wind turbines and other energy efficient products as easy as possible. However, you would still need to check what you can do with the local authority and there will be more consideration for flats, maisonettes and buildings in a conservation area or area of natural beauty.

For most solar panels, planning is not required as long as they are a 'standard' design, don't impact dramatically on the roof or project beyond the slope. Most solar panel companies will help to advise you on what is required – but always double-check with your local authority before you go ahead.

Currently things like wind turbines require planning permission. However, this is likely to change in the next year or so, so check with your local planning office. The planning office will be concerned with the height and dimensions of the turbine and where you are going to put it – on the property or in the garden – as well as the potential noise.

Minor changes

As long as you are not in a special area or in a block of flats, you can add satellite dishes and re-render or clad your home.

However, you need to ensure that, where possible, any antenna is placed in an area that is 'unseen' from the highway.

Internal changes (except listed properties), such as decoration, do not need any planning permission. Most things can also be demolished, as long

Property tips

- It doesn't cost anything to get a view from your local planning department on the home improvements you want to make. Visit www.planningportal.gov.uk and use their 'visual guide for homeowners' to be sure you don't need their permission, then if you have any doubts or questions contact your planning office. Where necessary they will also visit your property free of charge and put their thoughts in writing.
- You can also obtain a 'Lawful Planning Certificate' from your local council. This can be granted for a property that has previously been altered but where no evidence exists to suggest that planning permission was ever sought and gained.
- More importantly, if you are planning any developments and want to be 100 per cent sure that planning permission is not required, then you can gain a certificate as proof that your home improvements are legal.

as they belong to you and no one else is affected. However, for health and safety reasons, make sure they are done within the law and it's always advisable to check with the planning office that you can demolish all or part of a building.

WHEN PLANNING PERMISSION IS REQUIRED

In the main, planning permission is required when there is a dramatic change to the exterior of a property or a road, or when vehicle access is affected. It is also required where the work impacts on the community from a health and safety perspective, or where a certain look and feel needs to be retained or to be in keeping with the environment. If you are planning on doing any of the following work to your property, always check with the planning department before going any further.

Change of use

If you are likely to be dramatically changing the way you use a property, particularly one that is currently a business that you want to convert into

Even if your plans are passed by the planning department, you can't necessarily go ahead with the build exactly as the signed-off plans are constructed. Any plans passed by the planning department must then be checked and passed by the building regulations officer at various stages of the build (see pages 66-72).

residential premises, then you have to apply for planning permission. The same applies vice versa, if you buy a home and then convert it into a B&B or a transport depot, or anything that will involve an increase in traffic and people to and from the property. The main reason for this is that it may have an adverse effect on the neighbourhood and you are likely to have to pay local taxes for business premises, rather than the domestic council tax.

Household extensions (not applicable to flats)

The first thing to check is whether the property has had any previous extensions, which will affect your permitted development rights (see page 54). If the property has been previously extended, it is wise to contact the planning office and ask how much you can extend, prior to creating your plans to submit for planning permission. If you

Check it out

You must, where required, gain planning permission before you start a project. If you do not, then the planning rules can be very harsh – and they can ask you to take down whatever it is you have done, at your own cost.

haven't been in your property for long, it may also be worth asking if there have been planning applications for your property before.

Outbuildings in the garden

As long as you are not creating a new dwelling or somewhere where people would live/sleep, then most outbuildings are accepted without planning permission. However, if you are considering anything that exceeds a height of 3m, you will need to check with your local planning office whether you will be allowed to build. You also need to seek planning advice if you are creating anything that will cover more than 50 per cent of the garden area.

Adding a garage/off-road parking

Planning permission requirements in this area do vary, so it's important to check with your local authority. For example, you would normally need planning permission if a garage were expected to exceed 30sq m. Planning permission especially applies if you are hoping to create a two-storey building with a room on the top to use as a dwelling, such as an office, extra bedroom or playroom. If the garage is to be built more than 5m from the property and/or closer than 2m to a public highway, planning permission may be required. If you do get approval, there is then no cubic restriction as long as you don't exceed building anything that is more than 50 per cent of your garden space.

Converting a loft, garage or outbuilding

Usually, the only time you need planning permission is if the conversion exceeds the current roof height or adds more space than you are allowed. As long as the conversion doesn't change the overall dimensions outwards and upwards, you are likely not to need planning permission (unless it is a listed property or within a designated area such as a conservation area). However, if you are going to change the external look and feel of the property and dramatically increase the space, say taking a loft to a two-bedroom conversion rather than an additional space for storage or a mini office, seek planning advice.

If you don't get formal approval, you can fall foul of the Property Misdescriptions Act when selling a property. For example, if a loft is converted to add a fourth bedroom and there is no formal planning approval, then it can only be sold as a 'three-bedroom property with a converted loft'. This can dramatically impact on the price of a property, so it's not worth skimping on gaining approval.

❝ Most outbuildings are accepted without planning permission as long as you are not creating a new dwelling. ❞

Boundaries

You only need to apply for planning permission if you are building a boundary, such as a timber fence or hedge, that is over 2m high or 1m when alongside a pavement, road or other public highway, or you are in a listed property or an area where you have to gain permission for the type of boundary you are erecting. Seek advice from your local planning office.

We have also heard much about the leylandii trees that people plant to quickly create a boundary. Although they aren't affected by planning law, the trees do form part of the Anti-social Behaviour Act 2003. Under this Act, a neighbour can complain if the hedge is over 2m high. However, if you are not disturbing anyone and are not near a public highway, then there are no real restrictions.

KEEPING TRACK OF PAPERWORK

At the time that you are involved in your property project, it is unlikely that the paperwork will seem that important. However, it is essential that you keep everything. This includes:

- **Copies of all correspondence** with the local authority (planning/building regulations) including before, during and post the works.
- **Dates and summary of any telephone conversations.**
- **Dates and summary of all planning/building inspector visits** (ask for any requests/comments in writing from an inspector/officer).

- Any certificates or guarantees for the work done.

One of the reasons it is essential that you keep this information is because if you move home, copies will be requested as part of the legal process. With the introduction of HIPs after August 2007, it is helpful if you can provide this information upfront in order to market your property. If you have made large changes to a property and cannot produce the relevant paperwork, such as a Building Certificate, or indeed you haven't adhered to the building regulations and made the changes requested, then a buyer may not even be able to get a mortgage to buy your property. So unless you keep this information safe, you may find it difficult to sell your home.

Property tip

When you buy a home, you receive lots of information about the property you are buying – and this should include any previous planning decisions and building control certificates. Other documents you may receive include guarantees for work on the property, such as timber and damp treatments or for new windows. Make sure you keep this information to hand, well filed and add to it any further papers for work that you do on the property.

Planning applications

When trying to obtain planning permission, first talk to the planning office before you do anything. Then, if required, apply for planning permission, taking into consideration the information and suggestions the officer gave you. Next, your application will be published and feedback gained and, finally, you either gain permission or not. If not, you may make amendments and re-apply or appeal.

TALK TO YOUR PLANNING OFFICER

This is a very important step. Anyone will benefit from taking the time and effort to show the planning office what they would like to do, especially if they give them information to help assess the potential for planning permission prior to applying formally. It doesn't mean that any rules will be bent on your behalf, but it does give you an invaluable 'heads up' of what you can and can't do.

Emailing your local authority is possible, but there is nothing like human contact and trying to build a working relationship. The best option is to ring and speak to someone within the planning office to find out the name of the person that looks after your area by giving them your postcode. Ask them what information you can provide upfront to receive their advice. It is likely that they would ask you to do the following:

- Lay out clearly in a letter what it is that you intend to do.

- Give an indication of what materials you are likely to be using, e.g. stone, brick, timber with PVC-U windows or wooden sash windows.
- Include a diagram of your property. Try to do it to scale and clearly indicate in a different colour to show what you are hoping to do, and where.
- Take photos of the whole of your property, the specific area where you are planning to make the changes and the surrounding area, such as boundaries that you have with a neighbour's property, the public highway and properties opposite or that have had similar work done to what you are looking to do.

Once you have received formal feedback, talk to your neighbours who may be affected by the work. Ideally gain their support or make alterations, if you can, that will help ensure they don't scupper your plans by putting in an objection that could have been avoided at the early stages.

APPLYING FOR PLANNING PERMISSION

Once you have had the feedback from the planning office, request the relevant forms to apply for planning permission. There are two types of planning permission you can apply for:

Outline planning permission

In the main, this is applied for for newly built properties, large developments or for very large changes to a property, so it isn't usually needed for private home improvements. Some people apply for outline permission initially as it is cheaper than applying for full planning permission and there is a fear that the latter may be rejected. If you have a listed building, then you have no choice but to go straight to detailed/full planning permission.

Outline planning is useful if you are not sure where to site a building – such as a garage – or if you need to establish a new access to a property. However, if you consulted the planning office, this should have been sorted anyway and you can always ask if this is an advisable route forward or whether applying for full planning approval would be better.

If you do apply and receive consent for outline planning, then you have up to three years to apply for full planning permission and at least start to build.

Full planning permission

This is the route that most extensive home improvements will need to take. To fill in and send off the form, you will usually need to include:

- **Contact details** (this may be yours, your builders or an architect).
- **An indication of what type of application** you are making.
- **Details of any changes** to access to the property.
- **List any trees,** buildings or part of the property that will need to be taken down.
- **Information about drainage** and external materials used.
- **Ownership certificate** (declares that you are the owner of the property).
- **Four copies of the form** and any additional plans/inclusions. You will only need to include a plan for major

---

Obtaining planning permission forms

You can obtain the relevant planning permission forms from your local planning office or download them from their website. When you request the forms, ask if there are guidance notes to help complete them. Each local authority can have different forms to fill in depending on what type of planning permission is required. For example, some councils have a special form for household extensions, others for changes to a listed building.

changes, change of use or new buildings. Send the plan on copies of an Ordinance Survey map showing the site with and without the changes. The scale needs to be 1:250 or 1:2500 and show the direction of north.

- **Fees form and the fee** (by cheque) (see page 65).

Although every local authority works differently, there are typically several stages to your planning application:

1 **Confirmation that the application is valid (within a week).** This is a fairly quick stage that checks the paperwork has been done correctly and that you have paid the required sum for it to be considered.

2 **Consultation (within 21 days).** This is where you see the white or yellow A4 signs in proximity to the property that is affected. They are usually attached to a lamp post, fence or similar. The local newspaper is also likely to carry a 'notice' section that covers a summary of the planning applications received. If the application affects neighbours, letters are sent to them too.

3 **Consideration (within two weeks).** A case planning officer looks at the property and the planned changes and takes into consideration any feedback received.

4 **Negotiation (within one week).** Where necessary, the planning department may ask you to make some changes to the application. This may require you to go back through stages 2 and 3 if major changes are required.

5 **Recommendation (within one week).** The application goes through a committee or an individual in the planning office for a decision. The planning officer will come back to you or your appointed representative, such as an architect or builder. In some cases, for substantial changes to a property, it may be put forward to a public meeting, which any objectors can attend. The case is considered 'openly', with a decision reached at that meeting.

Help yourself

Planning applications that get accepted and go through trouble-free within the eight-week timeframe are usually those that have been carefully researched prior to being presented.

Talking to a planning officer is a particularly crucial stage and people that don't get their applications accepted usually haven't taken enough time to check what can and can't be done and, more importantly, taken advice from those that are there to help prior to a decision being made. It is also a good idea to look at other properties in the street or in the area to see if they have done anything similar that would help support your application. For example, if you want to have a loft conversion with dormer windows – has anyone else done it? If you want to build a garage or outbuilding away from your property – has anyone else done this? Take pictures and send them with any application or when you are asking the planning officer's advice.

The most common mistake is errors on the application form, which delay the process from the start. So if you are doing it yourself, it might be worth sitting down with a planning expert, builder or local architect, even if you have to pay them for their help. It's good to get a second opinion from a professional and it's better than delaying the planning process and getting off to a bad start.

Many people also forget to send in the correct number of forms and plans that are required, so check and re-check that you have provided the right information for your area. Other paperwork that is often missed is the ownership certificate form, which declares that you are the owner of the property. Even if someone else is doing this work on your behalf, it is a good idea to check the application before it is sent, just to make sure you are happy and that they have fulfilled all the obligations prior to submission.

Another common mistake if plans are being submitted, is not using the correct colours for edging. The plans must show that the site for application is in red and the part of the area that you own is in blue. It is also important to ensure metric measurements are used. Unfortunately, feet and inches don't get you very far in the planning process!

> **❝ Errors on the application form will delay the process: get your form checked. ❞**

IF YOUR PLANNING APPLICATION IS REJECTED

The first thing to do is to take a deep breath and understand why the planning officer has made this decision. This should be detailed in the letter that you have received. It may be, too, that you have received planning permission, but there are conditions attached that you think add to the cost unfairly or make the work more difficult to do. You have up to six months to appeal against a planning decision.

Many people get everything right, then forget in all the excitement to sign the forms or don't include that all-important fee. So check, too, that either you or your representative have done both.

The Planning Inspectorate

Undertaking an appeal against a planning decision is not a straightforward or cost-free process. The Planning Inspectorate, who deal with appeals, can award costs to the other side if they feel you have just appealed for the sake of it, without putting forward a proper case, or if you don't conduct yourself appropriately during the hearing.

Appealing against the decision

If you do want to challenge the decision, it may be worth asking the planning officer if you could meet to discuss their decision and see if you could negotiate a compromise and then re-apply taking their comments into account. If this doesn't work and you still feel you have grounds to appeal, you need to obtain the appeal form (see box, below).

The critical element of appealing is to ensure that you show you have tried to adhere to the local authority's rules and regulations and that you have tried to negotiate a compromise. Although the agent's details will appear on the form, you need to ensure that it is you, the owner (or the 'appellant' as it is termed),

that is appealing and, as such, you should take as much interest and care in the appeal as you can.

At the same time as you are putting in your information to appeal, the local authority will be putting in their reasons for making the decision and any third parties that were involved (such as a neighbour) are allowed to put forward their comments too.

Once all the information is received by the inspectorate, they will typically visit your property, may have a meeting, say at the council offices (which you can attend if you want), and then they will put their decision in writing to you.

POTENTIAL NEW PLANNING SYSTEM

Although still in consultation, for England only, there is a review underway of the current planning application system for householders. The number of planning decisions relating to householders has doubled over the last decade and processing them is understandably causing an unsustainably high workload. The government believes that changing the rules will increase the number of permitted developments and therefore decrease the number of planning applications by over 25 per cent.

The changes intend to stop the current 'volume' restrictions, particularly for one-

---

Ways to appeal

There are three different ways of appealing – written, informal hearing or public enquiry. For most domestic home improvements it is likely that appealing in writing is best. It may be worth taking advice from a planning consultant or an architect who has specific expertise in appeals. These people may well be able to advise you on the potential costs of the process, so it could also help you decide if the appeal process is financially viable, or if you should go back to the drawing board with your plans.

 To obtain the appeal form, go to www.pcs.planningportal.gov.uk. You can either download it or fill it in online.

storey additions as long as the materials and roof structures match the existing building. This may mean fewer flat roof extensions, but could mean that larger extensions are allowed, depending on their nearness to neighbours and the highway boundary. Height restrictions, typically to the current property, will remain.

There are already specific changes being proposed to make more home improvements under permitted development. For example, for the government to achieve its policy of more sustainable homes, they are proposing that solar panels, heat pumps, wind turbines and other sustainable improvements are allowed – albeit with some restrictions.

Where the restrictions will be tougher, however, are changes to the roof structure – especially for loft conversions or adding another floor. The size of dormer windows causes many objections, so it is possible that loft extensions are more likely to require planning than before. As with extensions, it is proposed that neither terraces nor balconies are to be allowed under permitted development.

Other restrictions proposed are on outbuildings, which are mostly under permitted development. The new proposals suggest that only single-storey outbuildings will be allowed (including garages) and a tighter restriction is proposed on the total volume that outbuildings can take of the current garden space.

Finally, creating a 'hard standing', which currently has few restrictions, is proposed to be monitored and approved at local level rather than in line with national guidelines.

PLANNING APPLICATION COSTS

It is important to find out how much the planning application will cost as you need to make sure you budget for it. It is also wise to retain some monies, say £1,000–£2,000 in case you need to make amendments to plans, reapply, appeal or have to make changes to the build to meet the regulations.

For planning purposes, the amounts charged are given below. Check with your local authority the exact amount to ensure that you include this payment when you apply for planning, as they cannot progress your application without it.

Planning application charges

England	£135
Wales	£144
Scotland	£135
Northern Ireland	£225

To find out more about the government's proposed changes to achieve more sustainable homes, go to www.communities.gov.uk and search for 'Changes to Permitted Development'. The impact of the proposals won't be made known until the end of 2007.

Building regulations

Once you have gained planning approval and enjoyed a quick celebration, it is time to make sure you know about the complex building regulations that will apply during your project. Many people, including builders, can find this process frustrating. Sometimes you may feel that the rules are petty or being applied over zealously – and all at your cost.

However, bear in mind that the regulations have been developed, in the main, to ensure health and safety within and around the home. More importantly, whether you agree with them or not, you must have that Building Regulations Certificate to be able to sell your home, so it's important to comply.

As with planning laws and rules, there are building regulation differences in Scotland and Northern Ireland, so the information on the next few pages relates, in the main, to England and Wales. Where there are key differences for Scotland and Northern Ireland, these are highlighted.

Planning permission vs building regulations

Planning permission gives you the right to improve your home with the materials agreed. Building regulations are there to ensure that you correctly adhere to best practice with regards to the construction methods used to create the improvement. For example, although you care about the look and feel of an extension, as does the planning office, building regulations care about how the drainage works, that the foundations are safe and that if there is a fire in your home, new windows are big enough to ensure you can escape from the building.

This is why your drawings can be passed by the planning office, but you fail building regulations if you don't follow their rules and get checks at various stages. If this happens, you won't get a Building Certificate and may even have to undo the work done and pay to have it re-done correctly to gain your certificate. Without a Building Certificate for the work, it is unlikely that you will be able to sell your home.

BUILDING REGULATIONS: OLD AND NEW

Building regulations are constantly changing, so it is important that you consult your local building control officer with your plans prior to starting, as a new regulation may have come in that will impact on your home improvements. Building regulations affect most of the home improvements covered in this chapter and are often very detailed. For example, if you are extending a home or converting a loft, then areas that will be affected in the structure are things like:

- **Stairs,** to ensure they are fitted correctly.
- **Site preparation** to ensure the building is watertight.
- **Sound and other insulation** to ensure the improvement is energy efficient.
- **Fire safety,** such as smoke detectors and ensuring that escape from a window is possible.
- **Drainage and waste disposal,** ensuring that rainwater and sanitary waste is adequately taken away from the property.
- **Accessibility for the disabled,** such as ramps and doors that are wide enough for a wheelchair.
- **Gas and electric safety,** including the type of boiler and its fitting.

- **Glazing in windows** and how much they open, plus the ability to clean them – and escape from them in case of a fire.
- **Ventilation,** such as flues in the chimney and ventilation bricks, so condensation doesn't build up.

These regulations are listed under an alphabetical system and currently they run from Part A (the property's structure) to Part P (electrical safety), so watch out for the rest of the alphabet being implemented over the next few years!

If you are building an extension or a new building, then many of the building regulations will apply. However, if you are buying a property to renovate, then as long as you don't change the existing structure/systems, you are unlikely to have to make all the changes. For example, if you are installing an en suite for the first time, the building regulations will apply, and although this is also the case currently for taking out an existing bathroom and replacing it, most local authorities don't worry too much about enforcing this rule. As a result, you still need to double-check with a building regulations control officer before you make the changes. Equally, if a property has windows that don't currently adhere to building regulations, then you don't need to change them to fit, but you

You can check out the building regulations on www.labc.co.uk and www.planningportal.gov.uk. However you will need to consult an expert for your individual project to work out which building regulations you need to adhere to.

must make sure that any changes you make to the windows maintain the same level of safety. For example, they mustn't reduce the space that allows someone to escape.

As with planning permission, there are some buildings that don't require building regulation control. These include:

- **Detached buildings not normally occupied by people**, such as a garage, summer house or greenhouse.
- **Buildings for keeping animals.**
- **Small detached buildings** less than 15sq m floor area and with no sleeping accommodation.
- **Single-storey detached buildings** less than 30sq m floor area with no sleeping accommodation that are more than 1m from a boundary or constructed of non-combustible materials.
- **Ground level extensions** less than 30sq m floor area consisting of conservatory, covered yard, covered way, porch or a carport, which must open on at least two sides.

> **The building regulations control officer has no powers: it is down to the local authority to enforce regulations.** 〟

 The latest regulations may require that the improvements listed to the left comply with Part L regulations that define which 'thermal elements' of the changes need upgrading, such as insulating plasterboard or concrete blocks that help to insulate walls, ceilings and floors.

FINDING A BUILDING REGULATIONS CONTROL OFFICER

Unlike planning permission, the building regulations control officer is not always an employee of the local authority. They can be employed by the local authority as well as be approved inspectors, but both advise on regulatory requirements. However, they don't have any powers; it's down to the local authority to enforce the regulations. People considering basic DIY work that is not affected by building regulations would not normally be expected to employ approved inspectors, but may do so if they wish.

It is worth asking anyone locally, and certainly builders/plumbers/electricians,

Bath and North East Somerset have a useful checklist of what each part of the building regulations effect. Visit www.bathnes.gov.uk for more information, but always check with your own local authority just in case there have been any changes.

to see who they would recommend. Alternatively, visit your local authority website for people/companies you can use or visit www.labc.co.uk, which is the official Local Authority Building Control. This is an organisation created and funded by the building control service of local authorities throughout England and Wales. It provides help and guidance to those authorities and promotes local authority building control at national level. Most people, as with the planning office, will go through your plans with you free of charge before you apply and answer any initial questions you may have as this can speed up the process for everyone.

APPLYING FOR BUILDING CONTROL APPROVAL

There are two ways of applying: you either put in a full plan application if you are planning major works, or for most minor works or small extensions, you put in a building notice. A full plan application means the plans are looked at in detail and you are sent a formal notice that will approve your plans or make you aware of any problems that require the structure to be built differently. If you only need a building notice, this will be acknowledged in writing.

Although you as the property's owner are ultimately responsible for gaining approval, it is likely that your architect/builder/project manager will deal with this process – but make sure that you have this in writing at the start so there is no confusion. As it is you

Property tips

- Even if you think you are exempt from building control, don't assume this is the case – make sure you are. Ideally, get something in writing to say so from the building control officer you contact.
- It is important to understand that, just like planners, the building regulations officers are not there to design your plans, but will help ensure they have been draw up properly and advise if you are missing something that should have been considered.
- Building regulations apply to health

and safety and best building practice only. They do not deal with a property's fixtures and fittings, such as what the best type of paint finish would be for your new extension.

- As building regulations are so complex and constantly changing, it is advisable to always go for the full plan application rather than a building notice. As the LABC Director of Technical Services states, 'It is much easier to rub out a line on a drawing than be asked to take down a wall you've just built'.

that will potentially be held liable for any required changes, make sure you build a good relationship with the officer involved from when you start to plan your project. Don't just leave it to the professionals.

Full plan application

Full plans are often required for large extensions to a property as the structure, insulation, new drainage, protection from fire (including the ability to escape) and the stability of a new staircase need to be checked at different stages. This includes things like a loft or garage conversion, internal alterations that affect load-bearing walls, improvements that affect joists, beams and any other part of the home that impacts on its structure (for example, changes to a chimney-breast). They also apply to changes to a roof structure that may have a heavier roof covering that will require strengthening the roof trusses to accommodate the additional weight.

Feedback will take anything from five weeks to two months. Once you have received a letter advising that the plans are accepted or that you need to make amendments, you can put in a commencement notice, which informs your building regulations control officer of the day that work is going to commence. This must be sent two clear working days before work begins.

When you start the work, your building control officer will advise at which stages he or she will need to visit your property, such as checking foundations, drainage and roof structures.

Once the project is completed, provided you have complied with all regulations, a certificate will be issued.

Building notice

If you are applying for a building notice (for example, for small changes to drains), make sure this isn't just being done to avoid creating plans. The building control office will inspect the work as it progresses and may ask at certain stages to see plans or, worse still, may get work reversed and re-done if it's not to the required standards. It is a good idea to take photos of as many stages as you can so that the officer can see work carried out, even if it has been covered over. This is particularly the case for any underground work, such as drains or foundations.

With a building notice you get a certificate at the end as long as the building inspectorate has checked the work. Alternatively, it may be that the work is self-certified by the person who has carried it out.

SELF-CERTIFIED WORK

Many of the building regulations apply to gas, plumbing and windows. In these cases, people that carry out the work should be part of the Competent Persons Scheme. This is either achieved by a company employing the building inspector to sign off their work or by being part of organisations, such as CORGI (gas) or FENSA (windows and doors), which enables a professional tradesman to self-certify the work they have done for you.

New gas connections and gas appliances

For anyone to carry out work such as creating a new connection or fitting a boiler, or even connecting a cooker or fire to the gas mains, the work needs to by carried out be someone who is CORGI registered (see page 90). They will fill in the relevant forms and send a copy to you and to the local authority.

Electrical work

This especially applies when fitting a new kitchen or bathroom, as sockets are likely to be moved in an existing room, or created if it forms part of the new extension. This applies to outdoor electrics as well as electrics in new buildings, such as garages, porches and conservatories. So although you do not necessarily need building regulations to sign off for the latter, it is important that any electrical work that is done is carried out by a professional who can certify it complies with building regulations.

Plumbing

Most general plumbing work does not currently need to adhere to building regulations, apart from if a new boiler is being fitted or there are major alterations to – or a new – drainage system (rain or foul). Building regulations will apply if you are installing a hot water cylinder as these need to be checked to ensure they store water under pressure safely and that it is energy efficient.

Windows

Repairs to existing windows are free of building regulations, but new frames must be notified to the local authority and as long as they are fitted by a member of FENSA (see page 134), he or she can certify they adhere to the regulations.

FAILING BUILDING REGULATIONS

If you are asked to rectify work, depending on the issues involved, you normally have 28 days to put the work right. You can request a relaxation to dispense with the amendments on the grounds that the work does fit with the building regulations and that the request is really too hard or difficult to comply with. However, it's unlikely that you will be successful. It's much better to ensure that you don't fail building regulations by having plans checked before you start.

FUTURE CHANGES

For the future, there is a new Code of Sustainable Homes, which has and will continue to affect building regulations over the next few years. This ensures that all homes are built and adapted when improving them to be as energy efficient as possible.

To keep up to date with building regulations, visit your local authority website, www.labc.co.uk and www.communities.gov.uk and search for 'building regulations'.

The government is also consulting with industry regarding new regulations that will affect water efficiency and, in 2008, there may also be new regulations for the electrics in our homes.

BUILDING REGULATION COSTS

Building regulation charges are not as straightforward, or as consistent, as planning fees and you need to check whether or not the fees include VAT. As with planning, if you do not send in the right money, your application will be sent back and nothing can be done until the correct fee is received. There are three types of charge:

- For plans to be submitted and reviewed.
- For an inspection visit.
- For a building notice.

The first two charges apply for the likes of extension or conversion applications that will probably require payment for plans and the inspections. For the building notice, you pay the fee at the start of the work and it covers all the visits. The costs vary depending on the size of the alterations and each council.

The only way you will know the true cost of getting your building regulations approved is to check on your local authority website, as they set the fees. You can also contact the www.labc.co.uk or an approved inspector. It may be that the builder/professional who is gaining approval for the work will know the cost or can find out for you.

"New rules on electrics and water are coming into force."

Example of building control charges

This table gives average figures from councils around the country, including England and Wales, Scotland and Northern Ireland. To see your local and up-to-date charges, visit your local authority website.

Extension example	Plans	Inspection	Building notice
Small extension (under 10sq m)	£100	£150	£250
Large extension (over 40sq m)	£250	£400	£650
In Northern Ireland			
Small extension	£150 (£180 for regulation)		
Large extension	£180 (£216 for regulation)		
In Scotland (calculated on cost and called a 'Building Warrant')			
£5,000	£115		
£20,000–£30,000	£460		
£100,000	£880		

Developing a flat

If you own a flat, then you not only have to adhere to more complicated planning and building regulations, but also be aware of the leasehold agreement under which you own the property.

Even before you research the planning and building regulations that apply to your improvements, check your leasehold agreement for what you can and can't do. Similar restrictions also apply if you are living in a property run by a housing association. In this case, you will need to contact the association, preferably in writing, advising of the adaptations you want to make to your home.

When owning a flat, the 'outer' walls and communal areas are looked after either by a property management company, a residential committee or sometimes the owner of the freehold. Typically, they are responsible for the roof, what goes on the roof (such as aerials), the windows, jointly utilised cold water facilities (such as tanks), communal areas and drainage. The floor and ceiling structure is also part of the 'communal' facilities and any walls that you share with a neighbouring property will be subject to the Party Wall Act. It is the flat owner's responsibility to obtain permission from whoever their work affects as well as the local council.

Generally you can make the following changes to the inside of your property without requiring anyone's permission:

- Putting up shelves or pictures.
- General internal decoration, such as painting, wall decoration and re-plastering.
- Installing a new kitchen and/or bathroom.

If installing a new kitchen or bathroom, you are also likely to have to work on gas appliances and services, plumbing or wiring, but these are still subject to the same building regulations as for fully owned properties, and some regulations are specific to flats. Note that in properties built pre-1980, the plumber or electrician will probably need to have access to communal areas to turn off water or electricity. In this case, your improvements might mean that the water

 The Party Wall Act and its legal implications are described earlier in this chapter on page 52.

or electricity needs to be turned off and you will need to advise other residents well in advance of the time and say how long this may affect them.

Other improvements that you may require permission for from the leaseholder are a new front door or type of flooring. For example, some leasehold agreements now stop you from having wooden/laminate flooring unless it adheres to the latest sound regulations set by building regulations (newly built flats must already adhere to these).

In some cases, there may be tight restrictions on changing the internal work such as built-in cupboards, which, if removed, may be viewed as changing the internal layout of the building. This is especially the case if the building is listed or in a conservation area.

❝Some leasehold agreements set terms for wood and laminate flooring, and even on changing internal cupboards. ❞

Scotland & Northern Ireland

There are few differences between England, Wales, Scotland and Northern Ireland with regards to planning and building control. However, there are some areas that are different, and it's important to be aware of these.

PLANNING IN SCOTLAND

In Scotland, the differences from English and Welsh law are that:

- **You must advise and gain a certificate** to confirm that your neighbours have been informed of your planned changes prior to applying for planning. This certificate must be included in your application.
- **For houses,** the increase in space you can have is either 24sq m or 20 per cent of the property's volume, up to a maximum of 30sq m. This is a one-off grant and applies to the property and not each householder – since 1945).
- **No more than 30 per cent of the garden** is utilised for the extension.
- **Appeals** go to the Scottish Executive Inquiry Reporters Unit.

Building Warrants

Building regulations in Scotland are covered by a Building Warrant. A Building Warrant covers the same things as in England and Wales, but you can't start any work without a Building Warrant being granted. Other major building regulation differences are:

- **Additions to a property** that don't need a warrant are up to 8sq m and in some cases up to 30sq m.
- **If you are building a brick/stone wall over 1.2m,** you will require a Building Warrant.
- **You can install or alter the position** of a gas, oil, solid fuel or fixed electrical heating appliance and a certificate is not required. However, you still need to comply with regulations via a CORGI registered electrician.

 In Scotland, go to www.sbsa.gov.uk for more information and always double-check with your local authority verifier if you need a warrant or what regulations you need to abide by.

NORTHERN IRELAND

To apply for planning permission in Northern Ireland, you need to refer your queries to the Planning Service and they will refer you to the relevant divisional department.

In Northern Ireland, there are some key differences with regard to planning permission versus England and Wales. The first is that if you are extending the property via the volume limits, then any extensions built after 1 October 1973 are considered to have been deducted from the current property's size. If you are looking at extending further, your permitted volume development rights for extensions will be based on this calculation, not the current size of the property. No extensions beyond 115cu m are permitted without applying for planning permission either.

If you wish to appeal, you need to go to the Planning Appeals Commission in Northern Ireland.

❝ There are important differences in how development rights for extensions are treated. ❞

For more information on planning permission in Northern Ireland, go to www.planningni.gov.uk (the Planning Service) or www.pacni.gov.uk (Planning Appeals Commission).

Employing contractors

When trying to organise your budget, it is important to have quotes from all the professional organisations, such as architects, surveyors, builders and packaged companies (for example, loft converters and kitchen fitters). With the growth in buy-to-let and a robust house building industry, finding someone qualified to do the work you require may take some time. So, planning when to get the right people in will have a big impact on your home improvement project.

4

Contractors

A contractor is someone that supervises, manages and carries out a project according to what works have been agreed. Ideally, look for contractors that belong to a trade association, such as the Royal Institute of British Architects or Federation of Master Builders.

Contractors are worth considering as they typically manage the whole property improvement project from start to finish, including making sure the right people and materials are there at the right time. However, you do tend to incur a premium for contractors. Whether you employ a specialist contractor or

 Sub-contractors need to be managed by someone, either a professional - such as an architect, surveyor or project manager - or a builder or you.

Contractor costs

The figures given here are wide ranging as the cost of a contractor varies enormously depending on where you live and their level of expertise. Sometimes you might be able to negotiate a fixed cost for the job. The information here has been supplied in conjunction with www.mykindofhome.co.uk.

Contractor	Hourly rate	Potential cost on two-storey extension
Architect	£40–£200 or percentage of the cost of the project, usually 4-5%	£5,000
Designer's 'off the shelf' plans	£50–£100	N/A
Planning consultant	£50 or percentage of the cost of the project, usually 6%	£3,000
Surveyor	£75+	£200–£2,000
Project manager	£350/day	£3,500
Builder	£100–£300/day	50–65% of overall fee

Obtaining quotes

Most professionals will give you a 'no obligation' quote before you employ them, so ensure you discuss the financial aspect of the job. It is every bit as important as the actual work your contractors will do for you. Always ensure you get this in writing and if the prices start to escalate, ensure these are written down, too.

sub-contractor, such as a bricklayer or plasterer, depends on your time, your project management, organisation and problem-solving skills and your experience of home improvement projects. If you are working full time and haven't done an extension or loft conversion, then it may well be better to leave it to the experts.

ARCHITECT AND DESIGNER

Architects can be extremely helpful when looking at what types of home improvements would benefit your property. Many people take the decision to build an extension or convert the loft and then contact a builder or loft conversion company to do the work.

The difference an architect or designer can make to your property improvement is that he or she will ask you why you want to make the improvements, consider your ideas and may well come back with different options. These may be better from a budget perspective, may add more value to the home or even cause less hassle during the build process.

The architect or designer should also have a good knowledge of the planning and building regulations so he or she can help guide you from the start as to what you can or can't do to improve your home. This is particularly helpful if you are in a conservation area, area of natural beauty or have a listed property.

It is a good idea to contact an architect for projects that are likely to need planning permission, particularly any type of extension, conversion or major build project. The type of work they will do includes:

- An initial meeting to discuss your project.
- Preliminary project planning advice.
- Prepare the drawings.
- Submit plans to the local authority.
- Obtain tenders of work from contractors.
- Prepare the relevant contracts for above.
- Prepare a schedule of works and timings.
- Run the project.

It is your choice as to how much of this work you would like them to do and it is important to get a cost breakdown for the full service, then discuss with the architect what you think you would like him or her to do. It might be the case, for example, that both parties feel that the planning and building side are straightforward, so you can ask the architect to draw up plans, submit them to the local authority on your behalf and once planning is received, you will handle the work from there.

79

However, if the work is substantial and complicated (for example, a two-storey extension affecting a major part of the house and roof, costing in excess of £50,000), then it may well save you money in the long run to have the architect create tenders and contracts and help manage the build, as long as he or she has project-managed home improvements before.

Finding and choosing an architect/designer

There are three choices when looking for someone to help create your plans:

Royal Institute of British Architects (RIBA) To be a member of the RIBA, an architect has to have a degree in architecture and to have passed the professional practice exams. It is important that you contact a practice or architect that works on residential home improvement projects, rather than just commercial ventures or building new homes.

Chartered Institute of Architectural Technologists To be a member, an architectural technologist needs to have either a relevant degree or HNC/D. Once he or she has joined the institute, he or she can progress from an associate member through to chartered status depending on experience. A technologist

will help with your plans, timescales and costs, but is unlikely to manage the project for you. As with the RIBA, make sure that your designer has lots of experience in dealing with home improvement projects.

Design and planning company Some companies, such as 'packaged' companies who sell garages and conservatories, for example, either specialise in plans or produce the plans for you as part of the commission. As long as the home improvement is straightforward, there is no reason why you shouldn't use these 'ready made' or 'bespoke' plans. However, you should be aware that producing plans like this remotely may cause issues later on if you don't realise, for example, that there are problems with the land/property you are building onto.

To help choose the right person/ company for you, ask friends and neighbours who they have used or know – but make sure you like the work that's been done on their property first. Even pop a note through the door of properties that you like the look of (or knock!). People like compliments and to be asked, so they will probably be pleased to let you know who they used. Personal recommendations can be the best way to get a good service.

For more information about your architect and designer options, go to www.architecture.com and www.ciat.org.uk. Some websites for 'packaged' companies are www.garageplans.co.uk and www.easyhomeplans.com.

Ideally, brief and talk to three to five different companies/people, get some quotes and appoint the one that you believe will do the best job, will listen to you and help alleviate any concerns you may have.

Initially, when you contact an architect or designer, they should hold a brief meeting with you – which is often free. It is helpful to either have the meeting at your home or to take photos/drawings of your home (both inside and out) together with the road and neighbours' properties as well as details of who your local authority is.

Make sure that you explain why you want to make the changes and whether you want a return in the short or long term on the property's value. Who will use the new area and what for? For example, if it is to create a music room or office, the design considerations will be different to a kitchen or bathroom. Decide on whether you want the plans to be in keeping with or contrast to your property – you may want a contemporary look and feel that blends in with an old property, for example.

If you feel that the architect/designer really understands your project well and you can problem solve effectively together, you may be happy to let him or her get on with it, checking regularly on an agreed basis (e.g. weekly) and discussing any concerns you have, so that you can come to a satisfactory conclusion for any problems that occur.

On the other hand, if you want to keep tabs on what's happening, then you can be the person that signs everything

 It is essential to ensure that whoever you work with, you agree – in writing – what sign off is required for the design, monies and on-site decisions. Both parties need to understand how the project is being funded, the size of the budget, what the crucial finance stages are and the timings that need to be adhered to. Also, any flexibility that is available.

off. The upside is you should get what you want. The downside is that it may hold up the project if there are problems that occur during the day and you can't solve them, and you might be more tempted to make changes to the plans too often – resulting in increased costs and perhaps not the home improvement you were aiming for.

“Explain why you want to make changes and whether you want a return in the long or short term. ”

81

PLANNING CONSULTANT

A planning consultant can make the difference between getting approval or not if your changes are substantial or your property is in an area of conservation, involves a listed building, is designated on a flood plain or affected by radon. A planning consultant may also be essential if you have had your planning application rejected.

They will typically visit your property and give you a 'site assessment'. This is a report that explains how environmental factors (such as being on a flood plain) might affect your plans. He or she will assess your ideas and have plans drawn up that should get passed first time.

Basically, planning consultants should be experts in your area, know the local authority and understand the local planning nuances to ensure that when a planning application goes in, everything has been considered so it should get passed.

If you need to appeal, they will work with the local authority to understand what changes need to be made and work with you to ensure that you still get the improvement to the property you want and meet any restrictions placed by the planning authorities.

" A planning consultant can help you get planning approval. "

Finding and choosing a planning consultant

Planning consultants are usually members of the Royal Town Planning Institute and many become independent consultants having worked in local authority planning offices. As with all trade organisations, there are different levels of membership, depending on their experience and academic qualifications.

SURVEYOR

A surveyor is useful if you are considering a loft conversion, extension, re-roofing your property or anything that may affect the structure. It's no surprise that you will need a specialist surveyor for this, often called a structural surveyor (or engineer). They are knowledgeable about what is required from a building regulations perspective, so are able to advise you on what you will need to be aware of.

If you are using a 'packaged' company, only having plans produced or doing the project yourself, then asking a surveyor to help you is a good idea to ensure that you can do what you want and that the result is a safe structure that abides by the regulations.

A further surveying expertise is with party wall issues (see page 52) as he or she can advise on the legislation involved and help ensure an independent survey is

For more information on the Royal Town Planning Institute, go to www.rtpi.org.uk or for a list of planning consultants, go to www.rtpiconsultants.co.uk.

carried out so that the home improvements don't do any damage to neighbouring properties.

A surveyor will come and visit the property, go through your plans and advise on what issues the changes will require. He or she will also be able to give you likely costings for the work and some will have contacts that can carry out the work for you.

Finding and choosing a surveyor

Surveyors carry out many different kinds of work. Much of it is for commercial buildings and surveys for people buying/selling a home, so you will need to find a local surveyor that has experience, the time and is happy to carry out this kind of work for you.

You will need to work out what type of surveyor is important for your work – such as someone that specialises in structural surveying or one who is a party wall specialist. If in doubt, contact the Royal Institution of Chartered Surveyors.

❝On a big project such as a large loft conversion or two-storey extension, consider having a project manager. ❞

PROJECT MANAGER

A project manager provides an interface between you (the client) and the contractors and tradespeople as well as managing materials to site. He or she will either order the materials or work with the tradespeople to ensure the right material is there at the right time and on the right day – and is of the right quality at the right price.

A project manager should also deal with legal contracts and ensure that health and safety regulations are adhered to on-site. In summary they should manage the project from start to finish and ensure that a good quality build is created within the budget that you have available.

If you have a large project, such as a loft conversion or two-storey extension, and you are working full time with little experience of running this type of project, then it might be worth considering a project manager. Sometimes this role is taken on by an architect or the builder, which can work if they have done it before.

Some companies, such as large builders or specialist companies for loft extensions, automatically allocate a project manager to the work to ensure that it runs smoothly and that any problems are dealt with swiftly and in line with your requests.

 The Royal Institution of Chartered Surveyors' website is at www.rics.org.uk.

Some project managers may also do the preliminary work for you and then let you manage the project once it's up and running. For example, they may look over your plans, check these against costs and your budget and set up the contracts for you with the tradesmen you choose. On top of this they may provide you with a 'critical' path and project management document for your build, then you can manage it yourself.

Although there are no specific qualifications for a project manager, it is their experience, knowledge of materials and network of tradesmen that you are effectively buying into. As a result, you should ask to see what qualifications they have and what jobs they have worked on. It is likely that they started in the construction and housing industry and therefore should have some qualifications, such as an HNC in building studies, together with a health and safety qualification, such as understanding site safety and scaffolding.

Finding and choosing a project manager

Good project managers are usually in high demand and as they don't need any particular qualifications, the job can attract people that aren't so good. There is also no real consumer-facing organisation that they belong to, but you could contact www.apm.org.uk, the Association of Project Managers. You can go online and search for a project manager – especially ones that look after self-build projects, as they also take care of domestic extensions. Look, too, in Yellow Pages under builders and also contact the Royal Institution of Chartered Surveyors (www.rics.org.uk) as some surveyors have project management skills.

GENERAL BUILDER

Finding a good builder is essential. 'All-rounders' carry out all sorts of projects around the home from landscaping or re-roofing to smaller jobs such as fitting a kitchen (except the gas, plumbing and electrics) or building a garden wall. Most general builders are self-employed.

Finding and choosing a builder

When choosing a builder, whatever work they are undertaking, it is important to ensure that you make as many checks as possible, especially as there are not very many official qualifications for builders. The key things to ask are:

Do they belong to any organisations?
Organisations they may belong to include the Federation of Master Builders, the Guild of Builders and Contractors and the National Federation of Builders (see box,

Websites for affiliated organisations are: www.fmb.org.uk (Federation of Master Builders), www.buildersguild.co.uk (Guild of Builders and Contractors) and www.builders.org.uk (National Federation of Builders).

below). Organisations like these aren't foolproof as they are funded by membership fees and often take on companies because they want to grow their membership. As a result, they don't always make detailed checks before the companies join. Builders can also claim that they are members when they aren't or membership has elapsed, so always check with the organisation that they have a current membership.

What references can they give you? Make sure that the builder takes you to the work that he or she has recently finished and introduces you to the people who own the property. Don't just accept a written reference or call, as this method can easily be falsified.

What qualifications do they have? Qualifications to look out for are NVQs and HNDs in construction and especially some health and safety awareness, as this is critical for any building project and shows some thought on behalf of the builder. The builder should have copies of certificates of his or her qualifications to show you.

What insurance do they have? Ask to see a copy of the certificate(s) and ensure that the expiry date will cover the time they work on your project. There are three things that you need from their insurance: public liability insurance in case someone gets hurt on-site; cover in case there is damage to the rest of your property so they re-do the work or are insured to pay others, such as decorators;

that the work should be insured should the builder go bust or have an accident, so you can pay someone else to finish the job. If a builder doesn't offer all of this in his or her insurance, you can purchase insurance yourself.

Can you have a detailed quote? This is not easy to get from many builders. Some, even for building a home from scratch, will give a quote that is two lines in a letter! The best way to do this is to sit down with the builder, agree a fixed cost upfront or agree a daily rate of pay, and the number of likely days that the job will take. Agree a contingency plan should there be any problems during the build, for example an additional number of days/weeks that the work could take. Then go through the materials list that is required and work out prices for each – or even go to a builders' merchant with the builder and ask for costs and then see what you can negotiate off the cost. Again, build in a contingency plan for unplanned 'added extras'.

Ask for guarantees in writing. Ideally, the builder will guarantee his or her work for a period of time, such as 12 months, and it is important to get this guarantee in writing. Check on whether he or she will come back and do any necessary remedial work or whether you have the choice of being given the money to pay someone else to do it.

Ask to see a copy of their contract. This might be a letter or a formal contract, which lays out the work that the builder is going do, agree payment stages and what happens if there is a dispute, the builder can't finish the work or you can't pay for the work for any reason.

How you will pay for the work? Never pay for all of the work upfront. Make sure that you draw up with the builder a schedule of payment for each stage of the work (see page 100). Ideally, you should agree to pay when each stage of the work is finished to the specification provided and to your satisfaction.

 Depending on what workload a builder has, you could get lucky and find someone ready to start in one or two months if a job has dropped off. For really good builders, it could be as long as a year. Beware of builders that are ready 'straightaway', as this is one area that cowboy builders prey on (see page 94). Most good builders tend to line up one or more jobs at a time, to ensure a good workflow.

Builders and building regulations. It is essential that any builder you employ has a real understanding of the latest building regulations. He or she is implementing the plans that have been created so needs to know when and how you can deviate from the plans, but still adhere to the regulations. This isn't easy to check, but ensure that in the contract the builder has the responsibility of liaising with the building regulations officer and is there on the day the officer turns up to inspect the build at its various stages. Another way to check at the early stages is to sit down with the builder and the local officer at the start of the project to run through the plans for one final time. During a meeting like this it should be fairly obvious if the builder understands the latest regulations or not and if they clearly don't – then walk away!

❝Never pay for all of the work upfront. Draw up a schedule of payment for each stage of the work.❞

 If you don't know of a good builder through word of mouth, look in Yellow Pages, local newspapers and on online sites such as www.buildersite.co.uk or www.builderregister.com. Always check that these people are reputable by using the questions above and ensuring you have a good contract in place.

Sub-contractors

These are people that you either employ on a direct basis, or that an architect, project manager or builder employs on your behalf. It is worth understanding the work they can do, what qualifications they have and their costs so that you can decide whether to employ someone to do all the work or get a specialist in to do their bit.

BRICKLAYER

A bricklayer's job on the surface is quite obvious – they lay bricks! However, laying bricks isn't as simple as it sounds. Drawings need to be interpreted and calculations made for the number of bricks and how much mortar is needed. Bricklayers should also be qualified to fix problems with bricks such as pointing. Critical to a bricklayer's skill is to ensure that they build things to last and be level. In some cases, the bricklayer may also need – and is ideally qualified – to erect scaffolding.

Usually bricklayers are trained as an apprentice on a building site, but there are qualifications to look out for such as NVQs and SVQs and higher qualifications which have bricklaying learning options, such as a Diploma in Construction, City and Guilds training or some form of relevant construction award.

Finding sub-contractors

To find a sub-contractor, look in your local newspaper and Yellow Pages and ask around, especially people who have had work done or are in construction to see if there is someone that they can recommend. Ideally, find a sub-contractor that has been independently assessed, for example with NVQs or belongs to a trade organisation that has a code of practice and a complaints procedure.

> *“It is worth dealing with sub-contractors just as with contractors: get all the administration sorted out in advance.”*

 The National Self Build and Renovation Centre in Swindon has a list of contractors and sub-contractors. The centre also runs seminars and can offer professional help. Visit www.mykindofhome.co.uk for more information.

Sub-contractor costs

The figures given here are wide ranging as the cost of a sub-contractor varies enormously depending on where you live and their level of expertise. Sometimes you might be able to negotiate a fixed cost for the job. Materials will be on top of their work fee.

Sub-contractor	Daily rate	Specialist daily rate
Bricklayer	£100–£200	Stonemasons: up to £400
Groundwork/clearance	£100–£180	Drainage: £120–£180
Carpenter	£70–£150	
Plasterer	£70–£160	Lime plastering: £300
Electrician	£100–£150	Emergency: £40+ per hour
Gas installer	£100–£150	Emergency: £40+ per hour
Plumber*	£100+	
Landscaper	£70–£300	

* Plumbers often charge on an hourly basis as they are often called out in an emergency, so ask to be charged at a fixed rate. Hourly rates are £35–£55 for the first hour, followed by £30–£50 per hour.

GROUNDWORK/ CLEARANCE

This is one area of home improvement that many people forget about, try to do themselves (especially clearing the ground) or don't even know that there are companies that specialise in creating the groundworks for an extension to be built on top.

However, if you have lots of trees or a building/part of a building to demolish, it may be worth considering getting in a specialist. Ground clearance can take a long time if you try to do it yourself, and it may require specialist equipment that can be as expensive to hire as it would be to ask someone else to do the work.

Groundwork specialists typically undertake work that includes drainage repairs. They often carry out clearance jobs, too, and put in new drainage systems or prepare the land for works, such as building foundations. Many of the services they undertake include block paving or landscaping work, hard standing and bases for conservatories or garages.

 The Institute of Carpenters (www.carpenters-institute.org) and Timber Research and Development Agency (www.trada.co.uk) have lists of their members, which can be a valuable source for finding someone to work for you.

CARPENTER AND JOINER

Being a carpenter requires real skill in terms of translating drawings into anything from building a set of cupboards to fitting a kitchen and even creating a timber-framed house. The skill of a carpenter means dealing with accuracy when measuring, keeping things level and especially getting angles right. If your home improvement project involves, for example, a timber-framed garage or a timber office, then you may need to find a suitably experienced carpenter or joiner.

Qualifications for carpenters include NVQs and belonging to specialist trade organisations, such as the Institute of Carpenters. Joiners tend to be workshop based. They usually make the window frames, staircases, doors and other sometimes complex structures that carpenters then take on site and fit. You may well visit a joinery shop if you are having bespoke furniture or fittings made.

PLASTERER

Plastering is an extremely skilled job and plasterers are also usually trained in fitting plasterboard partition walls and can render external walls. Many plasterers learn as an apprentice on a building site or some have specialist qualifications, such as an NVQ or City and Guilds in plastering. Others may have gone on a private course to learn plastering, in which case make sure your plasterer has

on-site experience and you are not his or her first customer!

One of the main things to remember about plasterers is that their work is a messy one, so ask how they are going to keep your home clean and how they are going to stop traipsing plaster about the place while the work is carrying on.

ELECTRICIAN

Recent changes in the law (see page 105) mean that electricians need to do more in your home than before. They also have a new responsibility in that they must do official checks on all the electrics around the home, or the ones that they have worked on for you, and then give a certificate that confirms the work meets electrical safety standards.

The work electricians do varies from re-wiring a home from top to bottom to adding a new socket or moving a light switch. They need to be able to read and implement wiring diagrams from architects and create these themselves. Electricians also need to be adept at chopping out plaster, drilling through walls, floors and ceilings and ideally working out the best way to create the electrical system so that as few wires are seen as possible. Where wires are showing, then they should come up with effective methods to hide them behind things like skirting boards. Electricians also take on work to install security or home automation systems.

The Federation of Plastering and Drywalling Contractors (www.fpdc.org) have a directory of their members. This organisation also has specialists, such as lime plastering for older properties.

Employing contractors

Electricians should hold an Electrotechnical Services NVQ/SVQ at Level 3 and be 'Part P Registered' so they can legally approve electrical work. Some may be working in the industry already via an apprentice scheme from years ago and may not have these qualifications. In this case, they must make sure they have their current work assessed and, if necessary, re-train to continue working as an electrician. It is important that your electrician is up to date with the latest regulations, so ask if this is the case and get written confirmation.

Check whether he or she is a member of organisations such as the National Inspection Council for Electrical Installation Contracting (NICEIC) or the National Association of Professional Inspectors and Testers. Although both of these organisations are voluntary, and the electrician has to pay to join, both allow their members to issue certificates for all work carried out (even adding a plug or light switch) in accordance with national standards (see page 105). Always check that their membership hasn't lapsed.

> **❝ To legally approve work, electricians must hold a Part P Registered certificate. ❞**

Property tip

Don't forget to check your insurance policy if you have an electrical or plumbing emergency as they may be able to cover the costs for you. You must contact them first, not after you've called someone and incurred costs as they often have their own tradespeople that they use in different areas.

GAS INSTALLER

Any work to do with gas requires a fully qualified CORGI-registered gas engineer and every person that is registered with CORGI carries an identity card. The work they carry out can involve installing a gas cooker or fire through to installing gas pipe work for a new boiler and carrying out annual maintenance visits on gas appliances to ensure they still operate safely.

A gas engineer has to have the necessary knowledge to safely install gas pipe work from the gas meter to, for example, a gas boiler located in the kitchen. This can include lifting up floorboards, drilling through walls and installing ventilation ducts through the exterior wall to provide ventilation for a gas appliance. The CORGI-registered gas

Visit www.eca.co.uk and www.niceic.org.uk for more information and lists of contractors.

installer may also be a competent electrician and registered with the CORGI building regulations electrical competent persons scheme. This enables him or her to install the necessary wiring and controls so the heating installation meets the requirements of the building regulations.

To be qualified as a gas installer/engineer they need to have studied and passed the N/SVQ 6012 and must have relevant units of the Nationally Accredited Certification Scheme (ACS) for individual gas fitting operatives. Their ACS qualification has to be retaken every five years.

It is imperative that you ask to see their CORGI ID card as some unscrupulous people claim to be a member and may no longer hold an ACS qualification or may never have even been made a member. Do not accept any excuses and check that the date on the front of their card is valid (currently the registration period is for one year and expires 31 March) and that the rear of their card stipulates they are entitled to carry out the gas work you want them to undertake. A date next to a work category indicates that the cardholder can no longer work on that particular appliance after the date stated.

If you feel uncomfortable asking for this, then call CORGI or go to their website where you can verify they are a registered member (see box, below).

❝Some unscrupulous people claim to be qualified but may not be. Also, check the date on their ACS card is valid.❞

If you smell gas

- Call the National Grid emergency line on 0800 111 999. The service is free and available 24 hours a day.
- If you are calling from a mobile phone, go outside first or call from a neighbour's property.
- Do NOT smoke.
- Do NOT turn light switches on or off.
- Do NOT do anything to create a spark.
- Turn off the supply at the meter, as long as you do not have to switch on a light to find it, open doors and windows.
- Wait outside for the emergency person to arrive.

To find out more information about CORGI (and to find a locally qualified gas fitter) visit www.trustcorgi.com.

91

PLUMBER

Plumbers need as much general building acumen as they do an understanding of plumbing as they need to follow instructions. For example, for fitting showers, a general plumber needs to be able to lay pipes, chop out plaster/bricks and tiles, drill through walls, ensure that a bath is level and lay large pipes for waste, such as toilets or other drainage. For this type of work, a plumber doesn't currently need any type of qualification. For example, they could have trained as an apprentice on-site or with another plumber. However, most plumbers have a City and Guilds plumbing qualification or an NVQ Level 2 in plumbing.

Another type of plumber is one that is able to fit a boiler and work with gas installations as well as water. Typically, these plumbers have a qualification level that allows them to work with electricity as well, or a colleague that is qualified to do so, and can certify that the work is accurate and safe.

To do this level of work, the plumber needs to be qualified not only in plumbing, but also registered with CORGI and one of the electrical organisations detailed. In addition, qualifications such as a Bpec in unvented hot water storage is required.

❝ There are different types of plumbers according to the work they do. Some do not need any qualification at all. ❞

 Relevant websites for the plumbing industry are www.iphe.org.uk (The Institute of Plumbing and Heating Engineering) and www.competentpersonscheme.co.uk (Association of Plumbing and Heating Contractors). In Scotland and Northern Ireland you can also visit www.needaplumber.org.

LANDSCAPER

Landscapers do a variety of jobs, from designing a garden for you and advising what plants to put where, to carrying out all the work, including lopping trees, building ponds and, in some cases, even laying a driveway or installing an outside tap. Some specialise in work such as the best types of plants for your gardens' soil, while others may specialise in garden ponds or water features.

Landscapers don't need any formal qualifications although there are a huge number of qualifications that they can have, ranging from an apprenticeship in amenity horticulture, which usually include NVQ and SVQ to Level 2, through to certificates and diplomas in horticulture and even a degree.

For those that continue to educate themselves in the industry, they can also be taught by the Royal Horticultural Society (RHS) and gain a diploma and masters. Often they will visit for free and some may even produce a design for free if they secure the contract to implement their recommendations.

For more information on landscaping your garden, see pages 190–8.

> *"Landscapers will often visit for free and some may even draw up a design for nothing if they secure the contract to implement it."*

Websites to look at to find out more include www.landscaper.org.uk (Association of Professional Landscapers), www.landscapeinstitute.org (Landscape Institute) and www.bali.co.uk (British Association of Landscape Industries). Well-qualified garden designers are likely to belong to the Society of Garden Designers (www.sgd.org.uk).

Staying in control

Paperwork relating to the work done on your property and any guarantees you are given are essential to keep in a file, with copies of any planning permission given or building control certificates. If you decide to sell your home, this information will help smooth the legal transfer to the new owner.

AVOIDING THE COWBOYS

There are several reasons why disreputable builders are allowed to carry on working:

- **People don't ask and verify references** by visiting previous clients with the builder.
- **A contract isn't signed.**
- **Three detailed quotes** aren't gained before work commences.
- **People don't appoint an approved contractor** or one belonging to a professional organisation – and don't double-check that they are a current fully paid-up member.
- **People go for a cheaper,** cash option rather than a properly invoiced job, which may include VAT.
- **Some people are not willing,** or able, to wait for a reputable tradesman.

The first way to avoid a cowboy is to make sure you don't encourage them!

Many people think they could 'see' this type of person coming, but you can't. They can fool the smartest of people. Often they are quite charming, enthusiastic about the work you want doing, always return your calls, visit quickly and tell you readily how much the job will cost and when they can start. The real cowboys will also appear to be members of organisations, in the knowledge that you might not check and some even produce fake ID.

❝ Cowboys can fool the smartest people. They can be charming and enthusiastic. Beware! ❞

 Another way of avoiding cowboy tradespeople is to look out for the government Trustmark scheme (www.trustmark.org.uk) – see also page 96.

Classic tactics that dodgy builders use are worth knowing about and looking out for:

- **They are unlikely to offer a contract** or sign up to one that you give them.
- **Anything they give you in writing** might literally be in their handwriting and is unlikely to give any detail.
- **They are likely to offer a discount for cash** and ask for some, if not all, of the money upfront.
- **A tradesperson may claim to work for a company** that has a good reputation – maybe their brother's or one belonging to another family member – but may be an appalling worker under their own steam and not have the expertise to deliver. That's why it is worth taking the builder you intend to work with to previous clients' premises to ensure that they are the person that worked on that project – under the guise of looking at the work they have done.
- **Give detailed work and quote** – then don't follow it.

Questions to ask to help avoid cowboys

Here is a list of questions to ask anyone that you are considering working with. Don't be frightened or worried about asking this many questions. A good worker will understand and should appreciate that you want to make sure he or she is the right person for the job. Please note that some of these questions need to be adapted for the relevant trade, for example, an electrician wouldn't

necessarily need to know the local planning officer.

- What qualifications have you got?
- Are you a member of an organisation – if so, which one?
- How do you keep up to date with the law/building regulations?
- Do you know the local planning officer?
- Do you know the local building officer/inspector – if so, have they ever asked to have work re-done?
- Can you provide a detailed quote for the work in writing, breaking down labour and materials costs?
- When can you start the work? Is there any reason there might be a delay?
- Can I see your contract or a letter of agreement (see page 97)?
- Do you have (and ask to see) insurance backed guarantees?
- Do you have other insurance such as public liability?
- When do you require staged payments?

Jargon buster

City and Guilds A training organisation that awards vocational qualifications

NVQ National Vocational or Vocations Qualification. It is a work-related award that is given based on skills, knowledge and competence from studying and on the job training. There are various levels that can be attained

SVQ The Scottish equivalent to an NVQ

• Can you supply three references of recent work and can I then visit them with you?

Obviously, you need to tailor the questions to the job in hand. For example, if you are having a major extension or build done, then you need to ask all the questions. If you are just having a boiler checked or a socket added, then make sure the tradesperson is a member of an organisation, their quote is accurate and they offer a letter of agreement and some sort of insurance (in writing) if something goes wrong.

The Trustmark scheme

The government Trustmark scheme has been developed to help the general public avoid cowboys. Anyone with this logo and who you can verify is legitimately part of the scheme, commits to achieving certain standards of work. To gain the Trustmark, they must have been assessed on their skills, signed up to a code of practice and will either insure their work or their certification allows you to buy insurance from them for the work they carry out. There are still areas around the country that are yet to be covered by all the different trades, but it is worth checking via Yellow Pages or the internet to see if you can find someone that is part of the scheme.

GET ESTIMATES AND QUOTATIONS

Getting estimates on paper from a tradesman is not easy! You have to be persistent or even draw up the estimate yourself from a conversation you have had with him or her and then ask him or her to sign it with you.

If it is work to fit a boiler or adding electrics, it's not too difficult to do. You need to ask for:

• Cost of materials – and the type used, such as the boiler.
• Likely time – in hours/days.
• Fixed cost or a cost per day for the work.

If the work is for a big job, such as an extension or a conservatory/loft conversion, then the trick with estimates and quotations is to try to match them up. Everyone has their own way of pricing a job and rarely will a builder price a job in great detail. On the other hand, some companies have specialist software that supplies detailed quotes.

The sort of information you need to know is:

• **Breakdown of the major materials,** for example costs of:
  – Bricks, concrete, drainage, timber
  – Windows, doors, ironmongery, locks
  – Kitchen units, worktops, sink, appliances, tiles
  – Bathroom suite, shower, tiles
  – Boiler, thermostat, pipe work, ventilation, system flush

- Breakdown of the labour charges: how many people, what contractors will be used, how many days at xx cost of each labourer per day.
- A recommended contingency for the work, and an agreement that if the costs are likely to increase for any reason, this is agreed before the workman spends the money on your behalf.

> " Both parties must agree on who does what, when and for how much. You're then covered if anything goes wrong. "

ORGANISE CONTRACTS

This is one area where most jobs that are likely to go wrong do so from the start – because neither party takes the time to agree who does what, when and for how much. It's a simple concept, but if your project is to succeed or if something goes wrong, being able to claim and get due compensation so you can finish the project to the standard you'd first aimed for is essential. For small jobs under £5,000 it is possible to sign a letter of agreement as opposed to a full-blown contract.

Letters of agreement

These are a good way of setting out the basics of the work to be completed. They should include:

- A description of the work to be done, for example, 'Fitting ten kitchen units, a 10m x 1.5m worktop, one and a half bowl sink and taps.'
- Confirmation of who does what: who is buying/organising delivery of the materials and who liaises with the local council – including building control.
- The price for the work and who is going to do it, for example, 'Job to be overseen by Mr Johns, utilising a contracted carpenter, electrician and plumber.'
- Confirmation of what building regulations are relevant to the work.
- Description of the qualifications of the people doing the work, for example, 'All contractors have the relevant qualifications to carry out the work, including NVQ Level 2 and the electrician is a current member of NICEIC.'
- How the work will be paid for – and at what stages, for example, 'Payment for the kitchen on proof of delivery and supply of an invoice, labour to be paid for on a weekly basis by cheque on supply of an invoice and in accordance with the price quoted.'

 If you are employing a qualified architect, it is more than likely that you will be asked to sign one of the standard contracts created by the Royal Institute of British Architects. Depending on the level of work, your main contractor will also be asked to sign a contract direct with your architect.

- **How increases in the project cost** will be dealt with, for example, 'If the price of the work is going to go above the agreed price, this will be agreed before the costs are incurred.'
- **When the work will be carried out** – the day to start and finish and what the contractor will do if either of these change.
- **What needs to be done before the workmen arrive,** for example, 'Remove old kitchen, empty the room of furniture, roll up the carpet.'
- **What happens if there is a dispute,** for example, 'If there is a dispute over the quality of finish, then 10 per cent of the job cost will be withheld by the client for rectifying any defects proved in the work.' Agree on how an independent arbiter will be appointed, who will pay for this (e.g. jointly cover the costs) and that the third party's decision will be final.
- **Agreement of what areas the workmen can access,** including toilet/wash facilities.

❝ Asking a solicitor to check the contract may cost a few hundred pounds, but it may be worth it if the job is costing thousands. ❞

Contracts

Contracts are legal documents and are a good way of ensuring that things go smoothly, and if there are any problems, then you have all agreed in advance how to solve them to everyone's satisfaction. If you can't, it also allows the legal process to independently assess the issues and come to a conclusion.

If a company provides you with a contract, never just sign it. Ask them to take you through the contract terms and conditions one by one. Ideally, get the contract checked out by a solicitor. It may cost a few hundred pounds, but if you are spending thousands, it is a small price to pay to ensure that you are signing something that protects your interests as well as those of the company working for you.

Information that should be included in a contract in addition to the letter of agreement outline above is:

- **The contractor's name** who will carry out the work.
- **His or her address** and contact details (during the day and in an emergency).
- **Company registration/VAT number,** if applicable.
- **The price of the works** and what they will do if extra charges occur, which should be to give you a warning beforehand.
- **What materials/equipment/plant and outsourced labour** the contractor/or you will supply. For example, you may be doing some of the work or ordering and supplying some of the materials, such as kitchen tiles.

- Start date and finish date for the work. Include any compensation/penalty fee/damages if they don't start and finish on time. This is likely to be an agreed figure on a weekly basis. This should also include what time they start and finish each day.
- What happens if the contractor cannot complete the work for any reason, such as he or she falls ill or goes out of business.
- The contractor will comply with all statutory requirements, local and national regulations and by-laws. Who will be responsible for making the required notifications and arranging the necessary site inspections (this is usually the contractor).
- The contractor will have – or take out – the appropriate public and employer's liability insurance.
- The contractor will make good any damage to your premises caused by the contractor, their employees and third party contractors at their expense.
- What happens if the work isn't up to the agreed standard or if the contractor leaves the site for more than an agreed number of days (say five working days) without a reasonable explanation. In these cases, you should only have to pay for the work done satisfactorily to date, less compensation or any additional expenses as a result of them leaving/or the problems occurring. Also add in a time clause as to when things have to be rectified by, for example within five days of notifying the company of the problem.

- How much, when and how you will pay the contractor and under what circumstances you can withhold payment and, indeed, what recourse the contractor has should you not pay. Try to include a clause that keeps retention of 5–10 per cent for at least a month after completion to ensure the work has been completed satisfactorily (see page 101).
- How the contractor and their employees will behave on site, for example, which toilet facilities they will use, what they will put down to protect areas they need to use to access where they will be working. Also, if they need to walk up and down your stairs to get to the loft, how will they be protected?
- That the site and areas will be cleared of rubbish on a daily basis – or at the end of the work – and how rubbish from the work or lunch breaks will be taken away. This is particularly important if the work is dusty and may affect the rest of the property, especially if you have someone in the family who is asthmatic.
- What guarantees will come with the work. For example, most timber and damp work comes with a 25-year guarantee; other work may be for a lifetime or ten years. Make sure there is also some recourse and the guarantee is still valid should the company not exist during the guarantee timescale.

Attachments to the contract

There are some other pieces of paperwork that should be attached to the contract:

- Specification and drawings of the work to be carried out.
- A copy of the required building regulations that the work will need to pass.
- Any certificates that will be required, such as gas safety certificate.
- Copies of the contractor's up-to-date insurance documents.
- Copy of the guarantees that the work includes.

Make sure that you both have a copy of the signed contract.

Where to find contracts

There are lots of places that you can find a contract to use if your contractor doesn't have one. These include:

- **The Federation of Master Builders** (www.findabuilder.co.uk): email them the name and details of the builder you are going to use – whether a member or not – and they will send you a contract back.
- **A local solicitor,** who will either have one that can be adapted for your use or will draw one up for you for a few hundred pounds. Make sure that the solicitor has some experience and knowledge of issues that arise during home improvements.
- **The relevant trade association** (see Useful addresses) and ask if they have a sample contract you can use.

WHEN TO HAND OVER MONEY

This is often an area of dispute and annoyance for both parties. Sometimes the contractor does the work to the standard contracted to, then the client doesn't pay, and at other times the contractor doesn't do the work as promised, leaving the client annoyed, especially if they have handed money over in advance.

As a result, it is essential to break down the payments – and from a client's perspective to only pay after the work has been done to their satisfaction. The best way to do this is to work with the contractor you are employing to go through the different costs of the project and each stage. For example, discuss what the material costs are week by week and when payment for the materials has to be made. Most companies, such as kitchen suppliers

 The Office of Fair Trading has a comprehensive document that explains contracts and any issues as well as what up-to-date phrases should be used for home improvements. Visit www.oft.gov.uk and search for 'Guidance on unfair terms in home improvements contracts' or contact your local council as some of them have a sample contract that you can use.

The only time to withhold payment is when the contractor is genuinely at fault and you can prove this by referring to the contract agreement. Never hold back monies from a contractor unfairly. For example, if 90 per cent of the work is finished to your satisfaction don't then only pay 50 per cent of the bill, unless it will cost you this much to get it finished.

conservatory, then that work is paid for at the end of that week.

Take time to sit with the contractor and discuss these payments. Your ideal solution is to only pay when the job is done and to withhold 5–10 per cent of the total bill for a month or so after the work has been done to make sure there are no leaks or problems. However, this is not always practical for a contractor and there needs to be an agreement that suits both parties.

Once you have agreed payment terms, make sure that the schedule is referred to in the contract and then attached separately to it.

or merchants, ask for payment within 30 days of delivery. It's also a good idea to ask if the payment can be made by credit card. This can be useful as not only do you pay after the goods have arrived, but most cards offer some sort of insurance policy if there is a problem with the goods – or indeed they never arrive, giving you or your contractor further protection.

Once you have worked out and agreed a schedule of payment for the materials, look at the labour costs involved. If the contractor pays these on a weekly basis, it's a good idea to match this with the work they have to do and then stage the payments accordingly. For example, if week one is clearing and preparing the site, then payment will be made at the end of that week providing it is done. If week two is building the foundations and walls or creating the frame for the

❝ Paying for goods by credit card offers an insurance policy in case they never arrive or are faulty. ❞

HOW TO COMPLAIN

If you are not happy with the work that has been done, the first thing to do is list everything that you are unhappy with, why you aren't happy with it and what you would like to be done about it.

Then organise a meeting with the contractor to go through your points one by one. During this meeting have someone there acting as an independent witness (such as a neighbour or work colleague). Ask him or her to make notes of the conversation and what the contractor agrees to do or not to do.

101

After this meeting, put in writing what has been agreed – or what you feel should be happening. If the contractor hasn't agreed to rectify the problem, you might decide that you are not going to pay, but will add to the letter under what circumstances you would be happy to conclude payment. At all times, make it clear what the problems are, taking and including photos if necessary, and what is required to put it right.

If you cannot come to an agreement with the contractor, refer to the relevant clause in the contract. If nothing happens and the contractor is part of an organisation that has an independent complaints procedure, then contact them with the problem. Call to discuss the issue and get further advice and then, if necessary, go through their third party complaints procedure. Alternatively, suggest a third party arbitrator who meets with both of your approval. If you do not know anyone that can help, contact your local Citizens Advice Bureau or the Trading Standards Office. As a last resort, contact a solicitor to take further proceedings or go to the small claims court if the claim is under £5,000.

❝ Make it clear what the problems are; if necessary, taking photographs. ❞

To find your nearest Citizens Advice Bureau (CAB), see your local phone book or go to www.adviceguide.org.uk. The website for the Trading Standards Office is www.tradingstandards.gov.uk.

Electrics and plumbing

When most people think about property improvement it's all about the finished product – a new bathroom or kitchen, a new extension or loft conversion. However, it is essential to think through the 'unseen' aspects of your home. This chapter looks at electrics and plumbing: the types of jobs involved, how long they take and whether you can do it yourself or get someone in.

Electrics

There are two things to think through for the electrics in your home. First, make sure your current electrics are in good working order and, second, establish that you can easily extend them or know early on that you will need to create another source of energy.

ARE YOUR ELECTRICS SAFE?

When you are looking at any electrical work in your property, whether it's adding a new light switch or socket in an existing room, extending the wiring to a new room or adding a brand new circuit, it's worth getting your whole electrical system checked. This is especially important if your property is more than ten years old. Nowadays we are using more electricity in the home than ever before: from all our labour-saving devices, such as dishwashers and washer-driers, to the electronic 'gadgets' like laptops and game stations. This activity increases the pressure on the electrics and, as a result,

you should have your system checked every ten years to make sure it can cope.

This check-up may take anything from a few hours for a one-bedroom flat to several days for a large property, but it's a wise investment as it makes sure that your home is safe to use and you are not overloading the lighting or electrical sockets. Checking the fuse box is up to date with the latest circuit breaker switches is an essential home improvement so that if something does go wrong, the system shuts down only what it needs to (such as lights in the kitchen or downstairs sockets), rather than absolutely everything in the home.

How to have your electrics checked

A qualified electrician (Part P) from an organisation such as the NICEIC (www.niceic.org.uk) will need to check your electrics (see page 90). They have specialist equipment and know the standards required to pass an electrical safety check. He or she will check to see if there are any loose wires, which may be live; look for cracked sockets or ones that aren't working; check that each electrical socket (including lighting) is in working order and if everything is working well from the mains to the fuse box to your appliances.

Having your electrics checked at the time you are considering doing any work means that you can receive an electrical safety certificate. This can help if you are considering selling your home in the future as it can be added to the new Home Information Packs (see page 49).

PLANNING YOUR ELECTRICS AND WIRING

It is essential that you know where your fuse box is and what all the different circuits are around your home. In this way, if the lights suddenly go out, you know where to go and can reset the trip switch if it's safe to do so. Draw a sketch of each room – not necessarily to scale – and mark where each of the electrical sockets, lights, TV aerial and phone sockets are. This helps you to visualise how easy it would be to add a socket or extend your wiring system, or whether you need a whole new circuit.

Whenever you are looking at having electrical work done in a property, whether it's for a new kitchen or just because you are moving the furniture around and need sockets in different areas of the room, try not to think just about what you want now, but what you may need at a later date. For example, if you have young children who will grow into teenagers, make sure there are plenty of sockets for their gadgets when they are older. As we get older, a socket on a wall in the hallway, especially near the stairs and the bathroom, might be useful to plug in nightlights so it is possible to navigate easily around the house at night time. Phone sockets by the bed as well as downstairs are a good investment for anyone living on their own, or as you get older.

A qualified electrician can do any of these jobs and if your project is a reasonably large one, your architect can draw up a detailed electric plan for you, should you desire.

❝ Try to think not just about what you want now, but what you may need at a later date. ❞

Don't forget that all new electrical work requires a certificate, so that it confirms to the Part P building regulations (see page 71). If you are going to carry out DIY electrical work, notify the local building control body beforehand to ensure that you do everything to the letter of the law. If you don't get building control approval, in the future, with the HIPs coming in, it may be difficult to put your home on the market (see page 49).

Average electrics for a home

To help think about what you have now and what you might need in the future, here is some information about the average home, which is based on a three-bedroom property.

Item	Electrical requirements
Consumer unit	Most homes have only one consumer unit with ten circuits Ideally, you should have a consumer unit that is less than 15 years old and has circuit breakers
Number of ring mains	Normally, there is a minimum of three ring mains: one for the downstairs, one for upstairs and one for the kitchen One ring main can serve up to 100sq m
Number of sockets/lights	How many you can have depends on how much electricity you are using. As a guide, bedrooms usually need two to four sockets, a kitchen or lounge approximately eight, depending on the number of electrical items you have
Requirements per room	An average room needs a socket for a lamp, a TV, radio/CD player, PC/laptop, telephone
Kitchen	Cooker control unit (usually includes a socket) Sockets for a toaster, microwave, kettle, fridge/freezer and radio/CD player Additional sockets for a mixer, bread maker, slow cooker/juicer, TV/DVD player, extra stand alone lights, etc.

LIGHTING

Whenever you are looking at making changes to your home, especially the electrics, don't forget to think about your lighting. Years ago, just having a main light in each room was more than acceptable whereas now, creating the right lighting for each room is an integral part of interior design. The basic principles to think about when choosing your lighting – and therefore your electrical requirements – are:

- The different uses of a room, such as a kitchen/diner being a study in the morning, somewhere for the family to eat dinner in the early evening and a place to relax with friends for late evenings and weekends.
- What level of lighting is required at different times of the day, such as:
  - a bright light for studying or working
  - a medium light for early evening family meals
  - some mood lighting for evenings with friends.
- How you can accommodate your needs within the structure of your home.

When installing downlighters in a ceiling, the light fittings must comply with Part B and Part E of the building regulations. Check the light fixtures packaging and leaflet to see what applies and then make sure you get a qualified person to fit them.

In some cases you may want maximum light, such as when working, reading or carrying out a hobby that needs strong lighting. In other cases, you may prefer to have lamps, spotlights or dimmer switches that allow you to create atmospheric lighting. Don't forget that if you have an old property, your choices will be more limited as the walls and ceilings tend to be solid, so fixing recessed spot lighting is difficult and it will be more difficult – and costly – to recess wiring into the walls.

TV AND TELECOMS ACCESS

TV points and being able to access the internet/phone from anywhere around the home is becoming increasingly popular. However, when you are planning your electrics, it is important to consider what sockets you will need for phones, such as digital ones, which need electricity, and also for telecoms cables that can have a wireless router attached nearby. If you live in a home with thick stone walls, wireless access from all around the house might be difficult to achieve, so you may need extra sockets to connect to broadband.

As a guide, look at including a telephone socket in the kitchen, study, lounge and main bedroom, with a TV point (as a good selling point for any home these days) in as many rooms as you can, or at least the lounge, study and main bedrooms.

Property tip

Look for socket converters that turn a single socket into a double and other adapters which, when plugged into a normal socket, turn it into a telecom socket. Of course, if you are having work done anyway, it may be much more cost-effective to have them done properly.

Time plan

Recommending a likely timeframe for electrical work is difficult due to the fact that every property's wiring is different. Electrical work often takes place in two stages, 'first fix' which is laying the initial wiring, replacing a fuse box or re-wiring and then 'second fix', which is fitting sockets post plastering or decorating. As a result the whole job might add up to a week, but be split into three days one week and then, two weeks or even months later, the next two days to finish the job.

Plumbing & heating

Checking that your plumbing and particularly your heating is working well is essential before you start to improve your home. Many people think that it's easy to first do plumbing and then deal with the heating, while others leave all the decisions to someone else. Whichever you are, it is likely that you won't have spent enough time thinking about these issues when improving your home.

WHAT YOU NEED TO KNOW

Unfortunately, most people only worry about making sure their plumbing is in good working order on two occasions. Either when the heating packs up during winter or when it leaks everywhere!

Alongside waterproofing your home from the outside and ensuring your electrics are in good order, making sure the plumbing and heating system are up to date is a crucial home improvement, energy efficient and maintenance issue.

Apart from creating a heating and plumbing system for new home improvements, it is important to carry out annual maintenance checks. If you are renting a property or planning to rent one out, landlords annual gas safety checks are required by law.

Annual plumbing/heating checks

You can carry out all of these checks yourself, except servicing the boiler.

- Annual service on your appliances.
- Check visible pipe work and look at ceilings for any signs of water leaks.
- Check radiators are hot at the top and bottom.
- If necessary, bleed the radiators to eliminate any air in the system.
- Turn on the hot taps to check the hot water is still coming through quickly.
- Make sure the taps aren't dripping and that they turn on/off easily.

 One of the most important ongoing checks to make is for carbon monoxide (CO) escaping from gas appliances. To warn a gas user of the presence of CO, CORGI advises that a CO detector with an audible alarm is installed. They cost £20–£30 and are available online and at DIY stores.

UPGRADING YOUR CURRENT SYSTEM

There are a huge variety of projects that you may need to undertake for home improvement projects. The most frequent ones are covered here.

New pipework

The pipes that run to and from the kitchen, bathroom and boiler and link the radiators are the main ones to consider upgrading. In many old homes, the pipes tend to be quite narrow and are often clogged with scale and sludge. These pipes were fine for getting rid of kitchen waste when it just came from a sink, but with a dishwasher and washing machine, sometimes in use at the same time, the pipes are likely to need upgrading at some point.

There are two common types of piping used in domestic properties: copper, which tends to be more expensive and takes longer to fit, and plastic piping. It is important that the correct type of plastic pipe is used, depending on whether it is for the central heating or for supplying water that you can drink, and that it is

Property tip

If copper pipework is fitted, make sure that the plumber (or you) change any galvanised water tanks (such as the cold water tank) as the two metals do not mix well and can cause corrosion.

fitted by an experienced, professional plumber (see page 92) as it can be prone to leak if fitted badly.

New radiators

Radiators can be bought in all shapes and sizes, ranging from modern to period in style. So replacing old radiators may not mean you have to compromise aesthetics by losing a period feature.

To work out what size of radiators you require, you will need to carry out a heat loss calculation, which is best done by a professional. The calculation depends on the size of the rooms, size of the windows and whether or not they are double-glazed together with the types of walls and floors and insulation method.

When replacing radiators, the cheapest and simplest option is to put them in the same place as they were before, as there is usually less new pipework involved. However, it might be worth thinking about whether the radiators are in the right place or if you could gain more space by moving them. For example, it might be that you have two radiators in a room along two different walls. A larger new radiator may mean you don't need two, and can heat the room effectively with just one.

Metal pipes

If metal pipes are used for plumbing in the kitchen/bathroom it is important that a competent electrician (see page 89) is consulted to work out what type of bonding is required, as metal fittings, such as a radiator, may need this.

109

Usually, radiators are placed on walls where the most heat is likely to disappear, such as under a window or on an external wall. If you are fitting new radiators, it is wise to invest a little more money in thermostats on each one (see page 112).

Fitting a new cold water storage cistern

The cistern is usually found in the loft and can be made of asbestos, galvanised iron or plastic. Its function is to store water for the plumbing system. Not all properties will have a storage cistern, only those that have indirect hot and cold water supplies.

Cisterns are not difficult to replace, apart from trying to fit them through the hatch, as they tend to be around 1.5m sq. If this is a real problem, one solution might be to have two smaller, interconnecting cisterns. So it's wise to get some professional advice and a quote. Typically it will take around a day or two to replace and fit the new one.

HEATING YOUR HOME

Regardless of how your boiler is going to be fired, it is a big job to install a new hot water and central heating system into a property and you will have lots of decisions to make regarding the layout of the new heating system and the type of boiler that you will use (see page 113). There are four ways to heat your home and your water, or you can use a mix. You may, for example, rely on your boiler for heating the home and the water but make the showers electric.

Mains gas

If you have access to mains gas for heating your home and water, it is unlikely that you would want to use any other method other than, possibly, electricity (see opposite). If you can use mains gas, you will also need to think through whether you want to rely on your boiler for heating the home and the water, or whether you would prefer a mixed system, such as a gas boiler, but make the showers electric.

Get advice

With regard to designing and working out what size of boiler and how many radiators you need, together with the length and size of piping and the best way to heat your water, get professional advice. It is very expensive if you make the wrong decisions and try to re-do pipework or replace a boiler that's not big enough.

"There are four different ways to heat your home and your water, use one or a mix of the options. "

Oil and liquid propane gas

Oil and liquid propane gas (LPG) is mainly used in homes in rural areas where main service gas pipes were never laid and it is now not cost-effective to do so. Apart from needing to have an oil or LPG tank in your garden, heating your home in this way is similar to mains gas central heating.

Electric heating

Another way to heat your home and water is by using electricity for night storage, convector or fan heaters. The benefits of this type of system are that it is normally easier to install and the initial installation costs tend to be less than a gas central heating system.

Night storage heater In the past, storage heaters used to be bulky and ugly, but modern heaters are far more compact and aesthetically pleasing and have been made to look similar to normal radiators. Some night storage heaters also incorporate a convector or fan heater so there is access to instant heat if needed. However, it's best to heat them using the night-time electricity tariff as this makes them cheaper to run. It then costs less to heat your home than it would if you used convector or fan heaters, which use electricity at the normal tariff when used during the day.

> **❝ If you install night storage heaters, it is best to heat them using the night-time electricity tariff as that makes them cheaper to run. ❞**

On most night storage heaters there are 'boost' controls to allow more heat out if needed, but the downside is that once the heat is depleted, the heater won't recharge until the night time. These heaters can also have thermostats built-in to ensure they automatically store more heat at night when it's cold and less when it's warm, thus maximising the efficiency of the heating system.

The downside of night storage heaters is that the end user needs to 'predict' the heating requirements for the following day. For example, if there is a cold spell of weather, the heaters will store heat and release it the next day. If the following day the ambient temperature is high, then the heat from the storage heaters will add to the heat in the already hot room.

 For an idea of how long it takes to install/re-do plumbing in your home, see the chart on page 204.

Under-floor heating This form of heating has recently become more popular. Flooring tends to be one of the areas where a home loses heat, so by having a floor-warming system, it may be possible to reduce your overall heating costs. Electrical heating is normally very quiet as there's no boiler. It can also be combined with other types of heating system, so you may choose to only have it in your bathroom when you come to refurbish, or in a new conservatory. There is normally very little maintenance required, unlike a boiler, but if something goes wrong, you are likely to have to lift up the flooring, which could be quite inconvenient and expensive.

Heating water If you are using electricity to heat water, it either does this via a hot water storage tank or by heating the water on demand, such as an electric shower. Hot water storage cylinders have at least one thermostatically controlled heating element and the water is heated either by turning on a switch or via a time clock. For large hot water storage tanks this can lead to long periods of no hot water while the water is heating, say following the running of a bath.

Thermostats

Thermostats can regulate the temperature of the central heating system and when it comes on and off. Whatever type of heating you have, it is important to consider what types of thermostats you are going to have around the home. They can make an enormous difference to your bills and they can help to avoid accidents by keeping heating on low when you are away, helping to ensure pipes don't freeze in the winter time.

Most homes have a thermostat for their hot water cylinder and one or more room thermostat, which can have an inbuilt programmable timer to start and stop the heating. Some of these can even be programmed for different temperatures at different times for every

Property tip

Make sure that you manage the thermostats around the house to give you the heating control that you want. For example, don't fit a radiator thermostat in the room where you have the thermostat that switches the boiler on and off.

Condensing boilers in Northern Ireland and Scotland

In Northern Ireland, all newly built properties need to have a condensing boiler fitted and existing properties need them from April 2007.

In Scotland, this is not yet a legal requirement.

Types of boiler

Which type of boiler you choose to install may, in some cases, be dictated by the amount of space you have in your home. Because it is such an important part of heating a home it would be wise to seek specialist advice from a CORGI registered heating engineer, even if you make your decision and then ask him or her to confirm if it is the right type/product for your home. Since regulations have been introduced to install energy efficient boilers where possible (see page 12), there are two main boilers to consider, regardless of the fuel that is used to fire them.

The majority of boilers are condensing appliances and, as a result, the choice of a conventional lower-rated boiler may be limited to a few selected models. C- or D-rated appliances will cost more to run and are not as kind to the environment as a condensing boiler. However, in exceptional cases it may still be possible to install a boiler with a lower C- or D-energy rating. Seek advice from a CORGI registered installer before purchasing one of these boilers.

Condensing boiler

These are the most efficient type of boiler available as, unlike conventional boilers, little heat is lost through the flue. Although more expensive than conventional boilers, prices have come down and any cost you pay upfront should be assessed over five years, taking into account the annual bills. To ensure the heating system is as efficient as possible, it is important to fit thermostatic radiator valves on individual radiators, a cylinder thermostat to control the hot water and a room thermostat to provide control over the heating.

Condensing combination boiler

Combination boilers are popular as they don't require a separate hot water cylinder. The boiler supplies your heating and instant hot water. It is important that the hot water output of the boiler is matched to the household's hot water requirements or else there might not be enough hot water for everyone. It is a false economy to save money by buying a smaller combination boiler than recommended as it will be unlikely to provide hot water fast enough and at the desired temperature. When using hot water taps, be aware that unless the combination boiler is correctly sized, sufficient flow of hot water may not be available at every hot water outlet at the same time.

Electric boiler

A recent innovation in the electrical heating market is the introduction of electric central heating boilers. If your electrical installation is suitable, the electric boiler can even replace a gas boiler as it can supply heat to a wet radiator system and is useful in areas where there is no gas. It doesn't need an annual check and is relatively maintenance free.

day of the week. Ideally you want programmers that have a battery back-up, so you don't need to keep re-programming them in the event of a power cut. You might also want to be able to control the heating and hot water separately.

It is also a good idea to have a thermostat on each of your radiators. Some rooms are warmer than others, and if you have a family, some may like their room warm, and others cool, so it allows everyone to have a temperature that suits them.

TIMESCALES AND COSTS

To refurbish an existing heating system can be done in a day or two, but costs and timescales will vary with the type of heating you are looking for and the size of the property. Most electricians and plumbers have their own 'favoured' systems they work with. This might be because they feel comfortable and experienced at installing them and they find them reliable with good back-up if they need help. It is wise, therefore, to strongly consider their recommendations, as going with something different may result in it taking longer as they haven't done it before.

However, it is always worth checking around to see what you can find yourself. For example, always check what price they are charging for a boiler or other materials such as radiators as some may charge quite a sizeable mark-up and you may be able to buy the goods yourself to save some money.

New boiler

In the main, fitting a new boiler will cost from around £1,200 for a small home to up to £3,000 for a large home, depending on what is there currently and the upgrading required. Normally it will take a day or two to fit, and it's a good idea to make sure you have a Friday free with the new system to allow any emergency fixes, such as a leaky pipe, before the weekend.

Central heating

Installing a new central heating and hot water system, will cost anything from £1,500 for electric systems to £3,000 or more for full gas central heating including a boiler, thermostats and radiators for a large property. This can take up to a week or more, depending on how much pipework is required and whether you are fitting radiators, electric under-floor or storage heating.

❝ Most electricians and plumbers favour certain systems that they are familiar with. ❞

Check out *Which? Magazine*'s Best Buys for heating equipment, such as boilers, to see which they recommend and understand what you are getting for your money – go to www.which.co.uk.

Planning a kitchen or bathroom

It's a fact that a well-planned kitchen and bathroom add value to a home, or at least help to sell it quicker. When investing in a new kitchen or bathroom, don't get caught up in its design at the start as the most important aspect is researching your options. In the kitchen, invest in good quality carcasses that will last, and if you need to upgrade, you only have to change the worktops, drawers and doors.

Planning a kitchen

When planning a kitchen, research is every bit as important as the design – there are many options out there to be considered.

Kitchens are the new 'lounge'. We prepare food in them, eat and watch television and even entertain guests in them. A well-designed kitchen, therefore, with plenty of storage space, lots of workspace and easy access to the fridge/freezer, sink and cooker is what most people want to achieve.

There are a huge number of things you need to do when planning a new kitchen. The fun bit of choosing a style and colour should come last – the most important things to know first are what can go where and just how much you want to spend.

❝ Many people spend more on the kitchen and bathroom than they need to. Budgets should match the value you are adding to the property. ❞

DO YOUR RESEARCH

Unfortunately, many people spend more money on the kitchen and bathroom than they should – or had planned to. Unless you are planning to stay in your home for a long time, it is better to spend on a new bathroom and kitchen up to the value you add to that property by doing the work. You might otherwise be tempted to overvalue your property, thereby making it more difficult to sell, or you'll lose money on the development.

You should also take time planning and researching your kitchen. Keep to a budget and try not to get caught up in the salesman's patter. Ideally, before you even go to a kitchen manufacturer, think about how much you can afford and write down everything you need. Then add a list of 'extras' in priority order.

Good kitchens do not need to cost a fortune. The building merchants, local kitchen manufacturers or specialist companies that just supply new doors, drawer fronts and worktops can save you thousands of pounds, but still give

 More than almost any other area in property development, your budget can run away with you in the kitchen. See pages 28 and 30-1 for reminders as to how to budget effectively.

Water and waste

Whether you are planning a kitchen or bathroom, knowing how the plumbing will be connected and how and where the waste will be channelled out is key to understanding what you can and cannot do cost-effectively. The more services you need to move, including electrics, the higher the cost for your kitchen or bathroom improvement will be.

a great look and feel. Don't forget, too, that this is a competitive area and you should negotiate with sales people as much as you can. Try to get the kitchen you want within the price you want to pay, then take it to at least three other companies and see how much they will charge – without compromising on quality. Once you have found a company that you like, if they can't reduce the price any further, will they supply any appliances for free? Or include the sink to get the deal?

> **❝ This is a competitive area and you should expect to negotiate on price and on what the supplier will include for free. ❞**

DESIGNING YOUR KITCHEN

Start your plan by mapping out on graph paper what your current kitchen looks like, especially highlighting where the electric sockets are, how these return to the fuse box and where the plumbing and waste pipes are. Add the windows and any other restrictions, such as a chimneybreast and doorway, and which walls are external or internal. If you have a boiler in the kitchen, highlight where this is and note what type of boiler it is (see page 113). Make sure you use metric measurements. Then measure things like the size of your crockery and gadgets, such as a breadmaker, juice extractor or even a TV, to see if they will fit into any new cupboards.

Property tips

- Decide what you like/don't like about your current kitchen. If the layout works, only change it if there is a real benefit – for example, it increases the value of your home. Think what you want to keep – the appliances, even the taps or the carcasses of the current kitchen.
- When thinking about your budget, consider how long you want the kitchen to last. If you are improving the property for sale or for profit, then only spend what you need to, rather than splashing out on something you'd really like for yourself long-term!

Some key kitchen statistics

This information has been supplied by the UK Metric Association - visit www.metric.org.uk for more information - and gives helpful guidelines when planning your kitchen.

	Floor kitchen unit sizes	Wall-mounted unit sizes	Worktops	Sink units
Height	72cm	72-90cm	2-4cm	15-18cm
Width	30-60cm	30-60cm	2.5m, 3m or 4m and cut to fit	76-95cm
Depth	Up to 60cm	30cm	Depth of cabinet plus 3cm overhang	44-50cm

- Keep the work triangle distance from sink to fridge to cooker at 7m or less
- Allow for a 40cm clearance between an open kitchen door and the nearest opposite unit
- Ensure at least 120cm clearance between runs of kitchen units
- Ensure that there is at least 40cm clearance between the worktop and wall-mounted cupboards
- If you have a room less than 180cm wide, you cannot comfortably use standard 60cm deep units. Some manufacturers offer 50cm deep units, but they may be difficult to combine
- Most unit doors open up to a maximum of 60cm. Dishwasher doors usually open by 60cm and oven doors by 50cm
- A typical worktop height is 90cm, although this will not be ideal for everybody. Ensure that the elbow height is a few centimetres above the worktop height

Appliance measurements

You can have either integrated or freestanding appliances. Integrated can give you more layout options, but if you move, it will mean starting from scratch in your next home. They are also more difficult and expensive to fix/replace if they go wrong.

	Cooker	Fridge/freezer	Dishwasher (full/slimline)	Washing machine/ tumble dryer	Extractor fan
Height	90cm	140-180cm	85/80-88cm	85cm	14cm
Width	50cm	50-60cm	60/45cm	56-60cm	52-90cm
Depth	60cm	56-65cm	54-60/55-63cm	52-62cm	30-60cm

❝ If you are thinking of selling the property soon, go for a kitchen with wide appeal, such as a Shaker or other wood-style design. ❞

Finer points

Once you have decided what you want to keep or replace, think through the decoration. Do you want or need new flooring? What about between the worktop and the cupboards? Do you have tiles and want to keep them or are you looking for a new style? All of this can add cost to your kitchen refurbishment.

Then there is the matter of the different styles that you can choose from. There are so many styles that the best thing to do is to get some makeover magazines or look in the kitchen retailer shops or DIY stores. Don't forget to include the merchants' specialist kitchen showrooms as well as a local kitchen retailer and supplier.

If you are likely to sell your home in the near future, make sure you have a kitchen with a wide appeal such as a Shaker or other wood-style kitchen

that suits your home. Alternatively, if it's a home that will appeal to the 'modern' market, it might be worth looking for a good value 'slick' kitchen style with drawers that shut themselves, good storage options and that all-important look-a-like or real granite worktop.

Property tips

- When budgeting for your new kitchen, don't forget to add extras such as tiling, new flooring, curtains/blinds and any decorating.
- Look out for sale times to grab a bargain – post-Christmas and pre-Easter are usually good times to look at buying a new kitchen.

 To find your local kitchen specialist, go to the website www.ksa.co.uk. This website also provides a planning service. For installing a kitchen yourself, visit www.diydoctor.org.uk.

BUYING YOUR KITCHEN

Kitchens come in all shapes and sizes, so it is difficult to give an idea of costs. Cheap kitchens can even be bought second-hand to save some money, but check it all fits well and if taking it from someone else's home, do so carefully. On average, people spend around £8,000 on a kitchen, but if you only have a small kitchen and do a DIY job or use replacement doors/fronts, you can get them from £500 to £1,000. For larger and more expensive kitchens, with new appliances and including fitting, costs are likely to be between £10,000 and £20,000.

Bespoke kitchens can cost anything from a few thousand pounds from a local manufacturer and between £20,000 and £60,000 or more, if really exclusive.

Don't forget that some kitchens can take a while from placing the order to

 Make sure that you don't give any company more than 25 per cent deposit before everything is delivered. Check the payment schedule before signing a contract to purchase and have the kitchen fitted.

delivery. Beware that mistakes can be made on deliveries – or measurements for bespoke kitchens – so plan a little extra time for this should you be hoping to get your kitchen completed for a special occasion, such as Christmas or a house-warming party.

❝ Allow extra time for delivery and sorting out any mistakes if you have a date by when you definitely want the kitchen completed. ❞

 To give you a rough idea of how much a new kitchen will cost you, there is a handy online calculator on www.smart-fit.co.uk/fitting.htm. Or call 01206 330407.

Planning a bathroom

Renovating a bathroom is not a difficult task as long as you don't end up changing it around too much. Adding a second bathroom or en suite has been estimated to increase the value of your home by 10-15 per cent. So if you are considering refitting your bathroom, it may be worth finding out if it would cost much more to put in a second one. Check with a local estate agent to see if this is a worthwhile investment.

CHANGING YOUR BATHROOM

There are lots of ways to redevelop your bathroom – far more even than a kitchen!

Redecorate and accessorise

This is the easiest approach. For example, if the tiles are looking shabby or the grout mouldy, you can easily sort this with specialist cleaning materials. You can also use specialist paint to get rid of any unsightly tiles and turn them into a more palatable colour or you can re-tile. Alternatively, look at a new system of 'board panels', which are basically waterproof boards that can be easily secured to the bathroom wall. They come in plain or patterned colours, some even giving a tile effect.

The next thing to tackle is the bath and or the basin. It might be that the bath just needs a good clean, or the taps and waste pipes need changing, which are not just easy to do, but also very cost-effective. If the bath is a cast

iron one and the ceramic covering has started to crack, consider buying a resurfacing kit or hire someone to do a professional job for you. This is a good idea if the bath is an original feature of a period home.

After this it is a matter of accessorising, whether adding a new shower curtain or panel or putting down a new floor and finishing off with a new curtain or blind.

> **Property tip**
>
> Protect the finish of new or cleaned grout with a grout sealer that helps stop staining and mould growth in the future - a great idea if you are planning to let the property.

❝ It may be that your bathroom just needs a really thorough clean to get rid of mould, and a few new accessories. ❞

Upgrade the suite

It is easier to fit a new suite or relocate the bath/shower/toilet or sink as long as you don't widen or change the existing pipe work. When choosing a suite, consider a bath made from acrylic, cast iron or steel. You might want to go all the way with a luxurious spa or roll-top bath or even create a wet room.

It is best to buy a bathroom suite as high a quality as you can afford but because of the vast choice of suites out there, it definitely pays to shop around. Look online, at the local DIY stores and local merchants as well as local bathroom specialists to ensure you get the best deal for your money. Try to spot special deals such as 'clearance' or other sale offers to get an even better price.

If someone is quoting to purchase the goods and fit them for you, always check what it would cost to have these jobs done separately.

 If you are remodelling your bathroom, update the bathroom to current building regulations standards, such as ensuring that any metal plumbing is earthed where electrics are earthed and that electrical fittings such as fans, sockets or additional lighting are created and signed off by a Part P registered electrician (see page 89).

"Fitting a new suite to the existing design is cheaper and easier than relocating the bath, shower or toilet."

 For further information on showers, go to www.diynot.com.

Buying showers

Before buying a shower, it is really important to see them in action. Make sure that the shower has all its working parts external to any tiles or the wall, so that if anything goes wrong you don't need to strip the wall, just change the part.

Bath/shower mixer

This is the type of shower you'd find on freestanding baths. The hose and spray are combined with a mixer tap and the temperature is adjusted through the taps. It's a cheap way of having a shower as it doesn't involve any extra plumbing, but doesn't always give a great pressure and it is sometimes difficult to get the temperature exactly right. (Cost: £50–£600)

Manual mixer

This is a popular and cost-effective shower that has a hose and spray coming out of a wall unit and a temperature control that combines the hot and cold water supply. These are cost-effective and need to be at a good height to help with pressure, but they require the hot and cold water supplies to be plumbed in. (Cost: £60–£300)

Thermostatic mixer

This is a manual mixer that has the advantage of a built-in stabiliser to self-adjust the water temperature. This is essential if you have children, older or disabled people in the house as the temperature and flow of water should not be affected when water is being used elsewhere. The only downside is that it is more expensive than other mixer showers. (Cost: £120–£500)

Electric shower

This provides water separately from the mains cold water supply. As with mixer showers, they have temperature and pressure gauges that can be adjusted. These are a good idea, especially for an en suite or second bathroom as they supply instant hot water separate to the boiler system. If anything goes wrong with the boiler, you still have one hot shower in the home. However, the mains pressure needs to be at least 0.7kg/sq cm and the pressure and temperature can vary against each other. For example, you can get a high temperature with less pressure, or a lower temperature but a higher pressure shower. You will also need an electrician to install/sign off the work. (Cost: £50–£200)

Power shower

This is a shower that is connected to an electric pump or one that is included within the shower package. The benefit of this shower is that both the pressure and the water temperature can be adjusted, giving you the optimum shower for you. However, you can only fit this type of shower if there is a supply from a cold water cistern and a hot water cylinder, so they are not compatible with a combination boiler. A power shower can use as much water as having a bath, so it isn't conducive to saving water. (Cost: £200–£700)

DESIGNING YOUR BATHROOM

When planning a new bathroom or en suite, draw out a plan as described for the kitchen on page 117. In addition, measure how far away the room or space is from the existing waste/plumbing and boiler. Then work out how much you want to spend, ensuring that you don't over invest in the bathroom if you want to recoup your money when you sell. Make a list of what you need as well as what you would like to have.

Take all your information to a bathroom specialist who can help design and plan your bathroom options. Make sure they keep to your budget and ideally look for a company that can give you a 3-D image of what your bathroom will look like to help you decide on the best design.

Once you have a few designs under your belt and are sure of all the products you want to include, check to see what you can get for the best price. Buying the goods yourself – with the approval of your fitter – can help to reduce the cost by several hundred or even thousands of pounds. If you are buying from a company that quotes for installation too, then check to see what it would cost for a plumber (and electrician where necessary) to do it independently.

Bathroom statistics

Note that these are a guideline only and relate to 'standard' fittings.

	Depth	Width
Rectangle bath	70-75cm	170cm
Corner bath	110-150cm	110-150cm
Basin	40cm	50-60cm
Toilet/Cistern	68cm	35cm
Shower tray	70-100cm	70-120cm
Bidet	48-55cm	35-37cm

‟ Buying the goods yourself - with your fitter's approval - can save several hundred pounds or more. ”

For more information on planning your bathroom visit www.bathroom-design-guide.com, www.diydata.com and www.ksa.co.uk.

CREATING AN EN SUITE

If you can create an en suite, or at least a toilet and basin, it can help add value to your home and make a big difference if you have a big family or when visitors come to stay. It is best to use 'dead' space as much as you can – and space that is near the current waste pipe. For example, it may be that you have fitted wardrobes in a bedroom that can be converted, or the room is big enough to be reduced in size using a partition wall.

Another option is to take space off two rooms rather than one, especially if the walls are partition walls, but make sure each room retains its ability to fit a single or double bed. If you are not worried about an additional toilet and shower being downstairs, look to see what space you could take from the kitchen/utility room or even from underneath the stairs.

To save space, look for corner sinks or toilets, smaller than average sized sinks and even small baths. Wall hung units can save floor space and use a towel rail to double up as a heater. Ventilation is important, especially if there isn't a window, so think about fitting a fan (and get it certified).

Planning a kitchen or bathroom

Property tips

- If you can't fit a bathroom or en suite due to a problem with accessing a waste pipe, then it might be worth investigating if you can fit a macerator. They can be noisy, but are worthwhile if it means you get extra flexibility. For more information, visit www.saniflo.co.uk or www.edincare.com.

- Whether you buy the products yourself or get someone in, it is worth looking at the guarantee, given especially for things like the grouting or sealant, which are costly if they don't stick or start leaking. Look for lifetime or ten-year plus guarantees.

> **&&An en suite, or at least a toilet and basin, can add value to your home and also make a big difference when visitors come to stay.》》**

If the amount of space that you have isn't very large look at these websites for more ideas: www.spacemakerfurniture.co.uk and www.small-bathrooms.co.uk.

BUYING YOUR BATHROOM

As with kitchens, the cost can vary enormously. A cheap bathroom suite can be bought for around £200, but then there are all the accessories to purchase from taps to waste, plugs and any new pipe work required, which can soon double this price. Fitting your own bathroom suite can save around 70 per cent of the overall cost, but you have to consider the time and complexity of the job before you decide to tackle it yourself – leaks from a bathroom can cost a lot of money to fix.

The average bathroom costs around £3,000, but costs can vary from a few thousand pounds to tens of thousands of pounds for an all-singing, all-dancing large bathroom!

 Once your new bathroom or en suite is complete, make sure you gain the relevant building regulations approval - including drainage, any electrics and ventilation and that any glass used meets the required safety standards. For more information on bathroom building regulations visit www.diydata.com and www.bathroom-design-guide.com.

Windows and doors

It is easy to get excited about an extension, bathroom or redecorating your home, while repairing or replacing windows and doors can seem daunting and feel like you are spending money because you 'have to', rather than want to. However, renovated or new windows and doors can greatly add to the look of your home and help maximise sales value.

Repair or replace?

One thing that is daunting about buying new windows and doors is that there are so many companies that want to sell to us – and not all have the greatest of reputations. But remember that investing in the best windows and doors you can afford helps change the look of your home, keeps the warmth in – and the rain out – and, most importantly, protects your home from intruders.

As a result, it is worth spending time thinking about the right windows and door(s) for you and your home, choosing the right company and then spending a little time maintaining them once they are installed.

CAN YOU MAKE REPAIRS?

Before you leap into researching new windows and doors, first check to see if they need replacing or if you can rescue them – which could save you a fortune.

If your windows/doors are wooden framed, it's surprising how damaged they can be and still be restored. There are lots of products on the market that will help fill in holes and cracks in the wood or you can just take out the rotten wood and replace it with new. You can then use special sealants to make the doors/windows waterproof again.

- **With period windows, doors or PVC-U windows,** it may be wise to get a specialist company in to do the repair work for you. They will be able to advise if repairing is possible or not and ensure that any work done, particularly on PVC-U windows/doors, maintains the warranty.
- **For wooden doors,** it is surprising how much a lick of paint, newly sealed joins and new door furniture from a letterbox to a door handle can make the door look like brand new again.

❝ Repairing rather than replacing windows and doors could save you money. ❞

 For advice on how to measure doors and windows accurately, go to www.upvcwindows.com.

Windows and doors are being advanced all the time, as are the regulations for fitting them, so make sure you are up to speed with new lock fitting, glass and window opening and ventilation regulations before you buy.

66 Look for windows that suit your property, while considering how much care they require. 99

Property tip

When budgeting to fit wooden doors, don't forget that you may have to have the bottom of the door shaved off to open and close it over a carpet or other surface. If it's a 'high security' door, you will also need to check it will still open as the door will come fitted in the frame.

OR SHOULD YOU REPLACE?

It may be that your choice is fairly straightforward in that you just want to replace the ones you already have. When working out which new windows and doors to fit, here are some top tips:

- Look for ones that best suit your property. Many an old property has been spoilt by sash or timber-framed windows being taken out and replaced with cheap PVC-U, which yellows very unattractively with time.
- Look around other people's homes – especially ones that are similar to yours. Take photos of ones you like and then compare them to the ones in brochures.
- Decide how much care and maintenance you are willing to do on your windows/doors. If choosing timber, then either you or someone else will have to maintain them with a coat of paint or two. Gone are the days though that this needs to be done every two years. A good paint or stain job will last anything from 4 to 8 years when applied correctly.
- Work out how much you want to spend. The prices of windows and doors vary dramatically, from under a hundred pounds to tens of thousands. PVC-U is usually the cheapest material and timber the most expensive. It is

Before considering fitting windows yourself, take a look at the DIY guide on page 50. It may be more difficult than you think.

worth spending as much as you can afford – while checking you are getting the best value for money. Don't forget that you don't need to change all your windows and doors at the same time. You can do it bit by bit, or the front followed by the back windows/doors.

- **Draw a plan of each room** where you want the windows fitted, including the window and door measurements. Make sure they are as accurate as you can, and either get someone else to check them or a professional. It's easier to measure the windows/doors from the outside rather than inside.

> ❝ You don't have to change all your doors and windows at the same time: you can do it bit by bit if you wish. ❞

Example pricing for windows and doors

Cost examples include fitting, but you can expect to save approximately a third of these costs by fitting them yourself.

	Two-bedroomed property (four windows)	Four-bedroomed property (ten windows)	External doors*	Internal doors*
PVC-U	£2,000–£3,000	£5,000–£8,000	£250–£800 each	£80–£250 each
Wood: hard	£3,000–£5,000	£6,000–£15,000	£300–£700 each	£125–£150 each
Wood: soft	£2,000–£4,000	£5,000–£7,000	Not recommended	£25–£100 each
Sash/bespoke	£3,000–£5,000	£8,000–£25,000	N/A	N/A

* All door furniture is extra

Types of windows & doors

The two most popular materials for windows and doors are timber and PVC-U, but there are other types, such as aluminium and steel. The latter are rare and usually only used where needed, such as for conservation areas or in listed buildings. With advances in technology for all windows and doors, it is worth considering which is the best for your home and your budget.

PVC-U

These types of windows used to have a reputation for being a 'cheap' alternative to timber-framed windows. Now, however, they are being recognised for their efficiency and ease of maintenance – and some are even being produced to give a 'timber' look and feel! PVC-U windows come in all shapes and sizes, standard or bespoke, and over the last few years, the industry has developed sash windows.

There are many places that you can buy PVC-U windows and doors at very low prices, but remember that the lower the quality of the material used, the poorer the security and the more likely it is that they will 'yellow' over time.

When talking to different companies, ensure that you are comparing like with like quotes and make sure that their products and company meet the following specification.

- **Pilkington K glass** or equivalent.
- **'Low-e' glass** with high thermal insulation and noise reduction to maximise thermal insulation and solar heating, preferably with 28mm double-glazed sealed units.
- **70mm frame thickness,** which should replicate the original window profile size and ensure the mastic line is less noticeable.
- **Fully welded framework** instead of screwed together joints to make the framework sturdier.
- **The frame is made entirely from virgin material** to ensure longer-lasting whiteness and colour consistency throughout the products.

 For more information on choosing and fitting PVC-U windows and doors, visit www.windowstoday.co.uk and www.thewindowman.co.uk.

- Metal reinforcement in frame chambers for strength to make forced entry more difficult.
- Any glazing beads should be on the inside so intruders cannot remove them and the glass from the outside.
- A locking Saracen shoot bolt and middle mortise bolt is included in each window opening.
- For extra security of doors, look for the 'Secure by Design' logo.
- All products meet or exceed the relevant British Standards, including the revised document L and F.
- Ten-year guarantee on all frames against faulty materials and workmanship.
- Independent insurance company backed guarantee.

Jargon buster

Low-e glass Specially developed glass that helps to keep the heat in your home, provides solar heating and insulates you from noise

Pilkington K glassTM Glass that acts both as an insulator and a conductor of solar heat to/from the home

PVC-U PolyVinyl Chloride – Unplasticised. A plastic material that is used to create doors, windows, conservatories and drains

Saracen shoot bolt A high-security hinge that can automatically secure a window with a deadlock and further locks at the bottom and top of the frame

 When taking out old windows and fitting new ones, always double-check that a lintel has been put in place to hold a PVC-U frame as this material isn't usually strong enough to support the bricks/stone above the window frame. Alternatively, see if you can get the window/door reinforced for added strength.

> ❝ Lower quality PVC-U has poor security and is also more likely to yellow with age. ❞

 For more information on timber windows and doors, visit www.timberwindows.com, www.doorwarehouse.co.uk and www.bwf.org.uk.

TIMBER

Just as PVC-U is trying to replicate the benefits of timber, so timber is fighting back to replicate the benefits of PVC-U in terms of lowering its maintenance. However, timber does remain a more environmentally friendly product and you can create almost any shape, style and colour of window. When choosing timber, bear in mind the following:

- **If you can afford it** and are thinking of investing for the long term, opt for hardwood rather than softwood. Treated well, it can last 50 years or more. However, wood should last for as many years as you look after the windows/doors and good companies will give a variety of guarantees against rot, the units and the type of finishes, which can range from five to ten years or more.
- **Look for frames that are multi-layered** as this helps to keep out any wet and stops the wood from warping and twisting, which is usually what causes doors and windows to stick.
- **Ensure they have effective security,** whether built into the frame, or added by you afterwards.

Property tip

Some doors arrive with the furniture already fitted, such as a letterbox or door handle. It is worth pricing these against having them fitted as this can save you money – and a lot of time.

ALUMINIUM AND STEEL

As with timber and PVC-U, both aluminium and steel windows have pros and cons. In some cases, such as in certain conservation areas or listed buildings, you may have little choice and need to use steel as you will have to retain the look and feel of the property when upgrading.

Both these types of windows have the major benefit of great security. They are so strong that most burglars won't even look at breaking into a home via these types of windows or doors. Because of the materials used they don't soak up any water, so tend not to corrode and so are maintenance free. Although they don't have quite the flexibility of timber, both steel and aluminium windows can be custom made.

However, they are more expensive then PVC-U and wood, and although there are efforts to make them more thermal efficient, they don't typically

 For more about aluminium and steel windows and doors visit www.fensa.co.uk, www.steel-window-association.co.uk, www.c-a-b.org.uk, www.theheritagewindowcompany.co.uk and www.duration.co.uk.

Windows and doors

perform as well as PVC-U and wood. Both also take up a lot of energy during manufacture and so aren't as environmentally friendly.

Aluminium and steel windows are a specialist production and installation, so make sure that any companies you see are a member of the Fenestration Self-assessment Scheme (FENSA) (which they legally have to be), the Steel Window Association or the Council for Aluminium in Building (see box, page 133).

Costs

PVC-U and poor quality timber-framed windows are the cheapest to fit, with bespoke timber frame, steel and aluminium windows costing the most. For doors, hardwood (for external) and softwood (for internal) are typically the cheapest. With regards to fitting, it normally costs £25–£35 for each window (depending upon size). External doors are usually fitted with a new frame to take advantage of the multi-point locking, and will cost between £50 and £60 to fit.

Good quality PVC-U and timber-framed windows and doors are typically the same price with aluminium and steel costing slightly more. Alternatively, look for a glass reinforced polymer (GRP) composite door, which looks like wood, but the material doesn't vary with changes in temperature.

If you are DIY fitting, you will probably save approximately one-third of the costs, but you risk not having a warranty on the products, which may help to sell the property in the future.

Property tips

- Any company that fits windows must be a current member of FENSA (www.fensa.co.uk), which should ensure that the company is up to speed with the latest building regulations.
- Other relevant organisations that a window manufacturer can belong to are Guild Approved Ultra Installer Scheme (www.ultraframe.co.uk) and the Glass and Glazing Federation (www.ggf.co.uk). Window installers can be a part of 'Kitemark': www.bsi-global.com.
- If you are in any doubt as to the veracity of your supplier, check out these associations.

Extending the property

Extending your property will always seem like an exciting idea. More space, an extra bedroom, an en suite bathroom or a beautiful new conservatory. Most people, however, don't take enough care when planning how to increase their space, or indeed give enough time to book the best contractors, who might be working months in advance. It is also important to go through the planning procedure, which at least ensures you have good plans in place for contractors to work from.

Planning an extension

Building an extension shouldn't be a 'quick' decision. It is a good idea to involve the whole family as everyone can think of things that might be important. If you know someone that has just been through it, or is even halfway through, then ask them to go through your objectives and spec with you – they may bring valuable insight or further things to consider.

Be clear about why you want to extend your home. Do you want more space for a growing family? Or maybe you require a home office? Then make sure there isn't a different option to create the extra space that might be less hassle, take less time and even cost less money!

- **Think about what you would use it for.** For example, you might want to add a conservatory or extend the kitchen to make it into a kitchen diner. You may be looking to add a room that is multifunctional, such as an occasional guest room, which you can use as a second sitting room or an office for the rest of the time. There may be different options of how to extend and it's worth working out the pros and cons of each.
- **Does the extra space need to be a certain size** for a specific reason? For example, you might be creating a games room with a snooker table and

need a minimum amount of space. If it's an office space, you will need enough room for a desk, chair, one or two book cases, and if you hold meetings there, then a table and chairs. If you are looking at creating a new bedroom, does this need to be double or single and will it have an en suite? Don't forget to include things like what appliances you are likely to need in the room so you can assess what electrics are required and how you would like to heat the extension.

- **Create a list of what you want,** dividing it into 'needs' and 'optional extras'.
- **Consider what 'spec' you want.** For example, how much light do you need – and should this be natural or not?
- **Consider how much of your home** you are willing to 'hand' over to builders and contractors. Most underestimate the hassle involved in such work. Your house will become a building site for weeks or months; it will be dusty,

 Budgeting is key to a smooth running project. For more information on the money issues relating to building an extension, see pages 28–37.

muck will get into places you can't believe it could reach; and problems are likely to occur that you weren't aware of. Typically, the longer and bigger the job, the more disruption there is likely to be!

- **How long are you prepared to put up with this for?** A month? Six weeks? Six months?
- **What if it goes on** longer for any reason, or you run out of money halfway through? What is your contingency plan?
- **What is your minimum and maximum budget** – and how much can you put aside for a contingency?

CONSIDERING THE ALTERNATIVES

Once you have considered your objectives, specification and budget, work through the alternatives, especially if the room could be located in different areas around the property. For example, you might be considering extending for office space or an extra room for teenagers to disappear into. But there are lots of ways of doing this, some of which are less hassle, can be quicker and may well be cheaper too.

Check that you are utilising all the rooms and space currently in your property. Many people keep a room as 'storage' for so long that they forget it could be used as extra space. Of course,

if you want a conservatory, this isn't much help, but if you are thinking about extra space to create an office, then all it might mean is tidying up this room, getting rid of the junk or storing it somewhere else, resulting in a cheap and fairly instant fix for the space you need.

Similarly, many homes still have a dining room and if this is used only occasionally, you might consider changing it into a multi-purpose room. To help, there is lots of furniture that has been specially created to be multi-functional. For example, there are dining tables that become snooker or pool tables and a range of cupboards and workstations can store files and a computer, which can easily be shut away whenever necessary.

Another area in the home that is often 'dead space' is under the stairs. This could be turned into a shower room and extra toilet, or some people turn it into office space. The latter depends on where your stair space is, as you are likely to need some privacy and peace and quiet to carry on with your work.

Converting outside space is definitely worth considering for a room that no one will sleep or live in, such as an office or games room. It is estimated that in the UK over 80 per cent of people don't use their garage for a car but for storage instead and if you are one of them, you might want to consider converting it instead of extending your home.

 If you need extra space for people to sleep in, you may need planning approval. Check with your local planning office and see also pages 53–9.

SHOULD IT BE SINGLE OR DOUBLE STOREY?

Adding extra space that affects the walls and roof of your property is a big undertaking and however much you think it will be easy, it just won't. Building work is stressful. There is dust, people traipsing in and out of your home, horrendous noise and there are likely to be problems that occur as it takes place that will need solving in a practical way.

The main decision that needs to be made is where you would like your extension – and if you have a choice. It is important to ensure the property remains balanced upstairs and down, especially if you intend to sell in the future. For example, it's hard to sell a property that only has two bedrooms, but three receptions downstairs or, indeed, four bedrooms upstairs, but only one reception downstairs. Try to see if there is a way of extending so that once it is done, it looks like it was always there, not an add on. For example, some people opt for a cheaper flat roof when to retain the look and feel of the house, a pitch roof would be better.

Equally important is how you can gain access to the extension – make sure that it is as easy as possible! If you are planning a two-storey extension, it is likely that you will have to lose some space on the second level unless there is a window to the side that can be replaced with a door.

So, when deciding between a single- and a two-storey extension, bear in mind that:

- **A single storey is usually easier to attach to a property** without changing its character too much. It also means that at least your upstairs – in the main – will be 'free' of mess, giving you some respite during the build. Apart from the reduced cost, it is usually quicker and more straightforward than a two-storey extension when gaining planning permission, following the building regulations and also from a build-time perspective. Access to your existing home is usually easier to create from a one-storey than a two-storey extension and any problems that occur throughout the build tend to be cheaper to fix than for a two-storey extension.
- **However, it may be worth considering – and costing – a double storey,** just in case it doesn't cost as much as you thought. It will give you extra space for the future and potentially add value to your home.
- **Alternatively, think about creating a single-storey extension** with a view of adding a second storey at a later date. It is also quite a good selling point to build the single storey with foundations strong enough to add a second storey. This may even increase the price if you sell with permission to build a second storey.

❝ When considering an extension, it is important to ensure the property remains balanced both upstairs and down. ❞

Neighbours

It is important to consider your neighbours and what effect your plans will have on them as, for example, they may lose sunlight or become overlooked. Think through the plans and how you could minimise the effect on your neighbours and talk to them before you take things as far as planning. If you have adjoining properties, you may be pleasantly surprised that your neighbours might be interested in extending in the same way and you could both reduce the costs. You'd need to draw up a contract between you and then with the builder, just in case one party has difficulties paying or you disagree on how to move forward with the project.

Finally, the local council is likely to want to keep the landscape as similar as it can, therefore what might seem a small consideration to you – taking down trees or hedges – can be a major consideration in your planning application. If you can, when looking at extending your home, try to minimise removing the number of trees/hedges that you have in your garden, particularly any that are near the boundary of the property which faces onto the public highway.

 If your neighbour rejects your ideas because they don't like change, use the planning office as an independent adjudicator. During the build, try to reduce the impact of noise on the neighbour's property. If they don't want you to carry out the project, they are more likely to cause problems throughout the build, which will only add to the stress.

❝ The local council is likely to want to keep the landscape unchanged. ❞

 Most local councils have leaflets that you can request or download to help work out what you need to consider when planning an extension. One of the most comprehensive is from East Riding council (www.eastriding.gov.uk), but every council is different, so make sure that you check your own local authority's information as well.

Key steps — Creating an extension

- Decide where you want the extension
- Work out your maximum and minimum budget, and how much you have for a contingency
- Create the plans (utilising an architect or designer – see pages 79º81)
- Run the plans past your neighbours
- Apply for planning permission and building regulations approval
- Make any required changes to the plans
- Appoint (with a contract) contractor/sub-contractors
- Agree with neighbours any times during the day you can start/finish the build
- Organise your current space to provide easy access for contractors and less disruption for yourself (for example, if you have a spare bedroom, consider making it a temporary sitting room away from the mess)

- Create the foundations, including drainage
- Build the walls
- Add the roof
- Put in the windows/external doors
- Create internal partitions
- First fix electrics/plumbing/telecoms
- Insulate the extension
- Finish the walls and plaster
- Install the heating
- Second fix electrics/plumbing/telecoms
- Fit internal doors, skirting, etc.
- Decorate and furnish
- Get appropriate certificates

During this time you will also need to sign off from building control (see pages 66–72).

EMPLOYING CONTRACTORS AND SUB-CONTRACTORS

Taking on an extension to your home yourself is an enormous task unless you have professional help or are experienced within the construction industry. As a result, you should look at getting in the professionals to help you. You have a choice of using a company to do everything for you from start to finish – including getting planning and building regulations approval – or you could bring in sub-contractors, from employing an architect to bricklayers, roofers and general builders (see pages 78–102 for more information).

 A great online tool is www.growyourhome.com. All you do is register, which is currently free, then you can put in the information, including demolishing a building and they give you an instant guideline cost. Other helpful sites are www.house-extension.co.uk and www.homebuilding.co.uk, which have case studies, including timescales and costs.

COSTS

Costs for extensions vary according to the types of materials you use and the size of the extension. Typically a two-storey extension will cost twice as much as a single storey as it makes the build more complicated. If you build a single-storey extension but twice the size, there may be, but not always, a cost advantage. *Which? Magazine* has recently conducted a study of single-storey extension prices that revealed:

- An average single-storey extension (3 x 3m, one window) could cost between £14,750 and £17,750.
- A large single-storey extension, perhaps with period materials and features, could cost £30,000 plus.
- A garden room (3 x 3m) could cost between £10,500 and £12,500.
- A two-storey extension will be anything from £25,000 through to £100,000 or more depending on its size.

> 66 A two-storey extension is likely to cost twice as much as a one-storey extension. 99

Most companies will give you a guideline calculation based on the number of square metres – but see also our ready reckoner on page 33.

Finding bricks and tiles

When you are creating a new wall or building structure it is essential that the new extension or wall looks like it was there when the property was built. This is especially true when choosing bricks for external walls and tiles for roofs. Fortunately, both the brick and roof tile industry are experienced in helping you find the right product as there are companies that will match your bricks or tiles to exactly the shape, size and colour, which includes making them especially for you. This last option is particularly valuable (if more expensive) if you have an old property, especially one that is listed. Alternatively, use the internet, where some sites have 'brick visualisations', or go to a local builders' merchant with a brick/tile sample or a photograph.

Some builders or extension specialists may be able to help match the bricks for you. Make sure they don't charge for this service, though, as the brick companies offer it for free. Also make sure that you ask them if the 'brick registration' discount has been passed onto you in the quote. This is where your name and details are given to a brick supplier for a quote and the company or person that refers that business gets a better discount that won't be passed onto another company.

Useful websites for finding bricks and tiles include www.hanson.co.uk (has a brick visualisation tool), www.jewson.co.uk, www.build-center.co.uk , www.brick.org.uk and www.brickfind.co.uk.

Other types of extension

There are lots of ways to get the additional space you need that may be a lot cheaper than building on the house – and this is by converting current space that you have into the room you need. It could be an extra bedroom for guests or children who are growing up fast, or indeed that almost 'essential' room required to make space for the technological age – an office.

CONVERTING A GARAGE (OR OUTBUILDING)

In comparison to creating new space, this can be an easy option with less hassle, as planning permission isn't always required. Even if it is, it is normally a straightforward process, with the main consideration being whether it will mean you have to park on the street as a result. However, you must make sure that the building regulations are complied with or your project won't get the required building certificate, which you will need if you want to sell your home.

The pros of converting a garage are that the job is more likely to be quicker and more cost-effective than building an extension. It will also be less hassle.

Key steps	Converting a garage
• Plan the layout of the property (utilising an architect or garage conversion planner) • Check on planning and building regulations • Check and if necessary re-do the damp-proofing • Make any structural changes that are necessary • First fix wiring (and plumbing/drainage if required) • Create a new floor/ceiling, including the required insulation	• Remove existing garage door (if you want to) • Replace windows and doors • Create access to the home, if required or possible • Improve wall/ceiling insulation • Provide a covering for the walls/ceilings (such as plasterboard) • Second fix wiring (and plumbing/drainage if required) • Decorate and furnish • Get appropriate certificates

Key steps | Creating a garden building

- Plan where you want the building
- Research where to buy a kit
- Decide if you want to create it yourself or get someone in
- Create a level concrete base/other levelling system
- Take delivery of the garden building
- If required, weatherproof it
- Create the building base
- Put up the walls

- Fit the roof
- Insulate (unless already done)
- First fix electrics/plumbing/telecoms/ heating
- Add any further internal wall panels
- Fit windows/doors
- Second fix electrics/plumbing/ telecoms/heating
- Install guttering and facias
- Decorate and furnish

On the other hand, you might need to go outside to access it from the main house, and will lose storage space for things like bikes and you will also need to check on the impact on the property's price.

GARDEN BUILDINGS

Creating a new building in the garden is another way of gaining extra space. So much so that there are lots of specialist companies that will not just sell you the building, but create the required foundations, erect the building, sort the electrics and any required plumbing. Typically, these buildings don't need planning permission as long as they are within the rules (see page 55). Many of the companies that do this for a living will be, or should be, familiar with the planning and building regulations.

The pros of erecting a building in the garden are that you could sell it or take it with you should you move house. It would be easy to erect and you may be able to reclaim VAT if it's an office. It is also easier to conceal noise from the house. On the other hand, it may not add value to your property and you have to go outside to get to it.

Costs

The costs depend on how big a building you are considering and whether you are going to build to your own design or buy a kit. If you are creating it yourself, you will need to pay out for an architect/ technician to draw up plans or buy one off the shelf. This will cost around £250–£500. From here you will need to purchase the materials and then

 To view some garage conversion plans on the internet, go to www.garageconversion.com, www.garageconversionsuk.co.uk and www.space-solutions.co.uk/garage-conversion.

143

either build yourself, or employ a builder or a carpenter if a wooden building. Depending on the design, it is likely to be a two-person job as it's heavy work.

If you are buying a kit, most garden buildings start from around £6,000 and range up to around £20,000, although cheaper versions are available. You may save a few thousand pounds by building it yourself, but you need to weigh up this cost versus your time and the finished product. For accommodation that you can sleep in, you are likely to pay more, and this can be from £20,000 to £30,000, but these builds are likely to require planning and building regulations.

> " Do you want a conservatory or a sunroom? It might make the difference if you need planning permission or not. "

Property tip

Get a fixed price for the cost of erecting a building in the garden as it should be a straightforward job and you don't want someone stringing out the build to get more money.

ADDING A CONSERVATORY

When thinking about adding a conservatory, you first need to decide on whether you want a full conservatory or a sunroom. Whichever you choose will make a difference in terms of style and cost, and it can also make the difference as to whether you need planning permission or not and what building regulations apply to the build. According to FENSA, the definition of a conservatory is:

- Not less than 75 per cent of the roof area is made from translucent material.
- Not less than 50 per cent of the wall area is made from translucent material.
- It is either unheated or heated by a system with its own and separate heating controls.
- It must be separated from the main residence by 'external' doors.

A sunroom that is added onto the current structure and, for example, has a roof other than glass, will not meet this definition and is therefore likely to be classed as a single-storey extension (see box, below).

Most people choose a conservatory because they want somewhere they can use all year round, and have the feeling of enjoying the outside, even in British weather. However, others prefer a

If you decide to have a sunroom rather than a conservatory, read the information here and for a single-storey extension (see pages 138–41). If you go for the folding door option, see opposite.

sunroom as they feel it is more in keeping with the home, and don't, for example, want doors separating it from the rest of the property. If it is not really extra space you are after, but still want to have a room overlooking the garden, it is worth considering converting an existing room into a sunroom. This can be done by replacing part of the external wall with glass folding doors, although bear in mind that there would be a lot of structural care needed to do this as the external door is bound to be a supporting wall for the home.

The folding door system is not cheap and can cost thousands of pounds for just a few metres in length. It may be that for a little more money you could gain extra space as well as the light that you are looking for by creating a sunroom or conservatory rather than going down this route.

If it is definitely a conservatory you want, consider the following:

- **Your choice of style,** ensuring it fits your home. Use the same principle as adding an extension – at the end it should look like it was built at the same time as the house. There are a huge number of designs ranging from lean-tos to Georgian, Victorian, gable and lantern (see box, page 146).
- **What shape you would like.** Conservatories are often thought of as just rectangular or square, but they can also be a 'T' or 'P' shape.
- **Its size.** This partly depends on what you want to use the room for. If it is for a dining room and you want to be

able to entertain six to eight people, you should be considering a room measuring 4 x 3m. When you are giving your ideal measurements to a manufacturer, explain these are the finished internal measures as the conservatory company may base their measurements on other criteria.

- **Type of frame.** There are several types of frame and, indeed, some bespoke companies may offer you a mixture, such as aluminium on the outside, but wood on the inside, giving you less maintenance hassle. See pages 131–4 for a description of different window frame materials.
- **Its roof type.** This can be made of glass (see page 146) or plastic, of which the polycarbonate sheeting is the most common. Make sure that any glass used is toughened and ideally is able to reduce the amount of heat going in and out. Also, try to ensure there is a 25-degree slope on the roof because they will 'clean themselves' more easily than shallower roofs.
- **What sort of lighting.** Usually, you won't need lighting during the day – unless it is very dull and dark! If you want to use the room in the evenings, it's worth choosing softer lighting, such as that given from spotlights, table lamps, uplighters or downlighters.

❝ The considerations for a conservatory are: style, shape, frame, roof type and lighting. ❞

Jargon buster

Gable conservatory A conservatory style that has a steep pitched roof giving lots of light and additional height to a conservatory

Lantern conservatory A period style that has two tiers with additional ceiling height in the form of a large 'lantern' shape

❝ View conservatories at your local garden centre or some of the many showrooms that are around the UK. ❞

Windows and glass

It is imperative to get the right type of materials and it is worth spending as much as you can to get the very best as this will help ensure you can use the room all year round and save on heating/cooling costs. The glass should be double-glazed, specialist safety glass and be able to keep the heat in, without 'over heating' the conservatory (such as Pilkington K Glass or Reflex Glass). Ensure that it is incorporate laminated glass for security and to reduce the sun's rays. It would also be useful if the windows could open and close as required. Make sure, too, that it is well secured with high standard locks and panes that can't be taken out of their frame.

Heating and cooling

To keep a more constant temperature in the conservatory, use materials specially designed to keep the heat in when required, and reflect it when it's hot enough. This means you need to check the type of glass being used and ensure that the conservatory base is well insulated.

Ideally, you could look at investing in an air-conditioning unit, which both heats and cools the conservatory. This isn't a cheap option, though (they cost around £1,000), and they have to be fitted by an electrician. Or you could heat the conservatory in a more conventional way, such as adding a radiator or convector heater. Other options are under-floor heating, which can be fitted with the conservatory, or oil-filled radiators.

The style of conservatory

There is lots of help available for choosing a conservatory design, both on- and offline in the many showrooms available. Online, visit www.conservatoryselect.co.uk and www.ultraframe-conservatories.co.uk. This last one allows you to upload a picture of your own home and then 'drop' in a conservatory style and see what it looks like!

Alternatively, many of the homes magazines, including *Which?*, often feature conservatories. If you want to view in person, your local large garden centre is likely to feature them and you can visit many of the different conservatory companies that have showrooms around the UK.

Key steps — Creating a conservatory

- Check planning permission and building regulations
- Clear the site for the base
- Relocate obstacles such as down pipes from the guttering or boiler flues on the house walls
- Create the base that the conservatory is built on
- Build up any inspection chambers that lie within the base area and fit them with double-seal covers
- Erect and secure the conservatory modules on the base
- Fit the external doorframe
- Assemble and install the roof frame
- First fix electrics/plumbing/heating/telecoms
- Glaze the roof, and ensure it has a weatherproof join to the home
- Fit the window glazing
- Hang the external doors
- Create an entrance, if required, to the conservatory from your property
- Second fix electrics/plumbing/heating/telecoms
- Add gutters, down pipes and connect into existing gullies or new soakaways
- Decorate and furnish

Property tips

- If you are fitting doors out to the garden from the conservatory, try to make sure they are at one end, or at least opening out on the garden (rather than into the conservatory), so that you maximise the use of the space within the conservatory.
- When choosing a conservatory company, make sure they are a member of FENSA (www.fensa.co.uk) and/or the Conservatory Association, or are a Guild Approved Ultra Frame Installer. Make sure that they have a code of practice that they adhere to. Ideally this should include a third party complaints procedure, which has the strength to arbitrate on a financial settlement, not just threaten to 'remove' the company from their association.

Information about planning permission and building regulations is covered on pages 53–65 and 66–72. Re-read the sections if you're not clear on what you can and can't do without obtaining the necessary consents.

Costs

Budget DIY conservatories cost from a few thousand pounds, while those that are of a good standard and fitted cost between £10,000 and £12,000 for a 3 x 3m conservatory. The cheapest designs tend to be the lean-to, followed by the Victorian, Georgian or gable. 'P'- and 'T'-shaped and lanterns can cost twice as much as they are more complicated and take more time to build. Extra special, large conservatories with all the features can cost in the region of £30,000.

Don't forget to add the cost of the furniture and any additional features, such as heating and blinds. These can cost thousands of pounds and the more you spend on your conservatory frame, the less you may have in your budget to equip it and actually live in it.

“ Don't forget to allow for the cost of furniture and extras, such as heating and blinds. ”

Extending up & down

Getting extra space from your loft or a basement is not for the faint-hearted - or anyone on a budget! Loft and basement conversions are hard work, especially as they affect so much of the home you live in. When extending out, you can 'hide' away in other rooms, but when you have no roof - everything is exposed to the elements and to create a basement means builders traipsing through your home.

What is essential when extending up and down, is to employ experts who do these types of extensions every day of the week. If they are good at what they do, they should be fast and thorough, give good guarantees for the work they do and have insurance policies should anything go wrong.

PLANNING A LOFT CONVERSION

Certain types of roof structures are much easier to alter than others, which will obviously affect the cost of the conversion. They can, in fact, be so costly that you might want to consider building a one- or two-storey extension instead to achieve your objectives. Of course, in a terrace property it may be the only cost-effective way of gaining extra space. Whatever you decide on, check with local estate agents/surveyors on just how cost-effective it would be to go ahead. This is especially important if you are not planning to stay for more than five years, as you may not get an instant payback. Indeed, in some cases it may detract from the value if it puts the property out of the maximum price that anyone would pay to live on your street. You should also consider the potential loss of storage space, unless you find a way to create space in the new loft conversion.

There are two ways of working out if you can convert your loft easily: by using websites that have Q&As or by going up in the loft and seeing if you can stand up! Then you should:

- **Consult a structural engineer** or someone recommended by a loft conversion company, who should have

 Sites that have tools to help are www.houseofopportunities.co.uk, which shows you pictorially which type of roof structures are easy to convert, www.econoloft.co.uk and www.loftsandattics.co.uk.

their own surveyor. Make sure that he or she is a fully qualified, paid-up member of the Royal Institution of Chartered Surveyors (RICS).

- **See if it's possible to site a staircase** to the next level – preferably off the current landing. Depending on the layout of your home, you may be able to go straight up from the stairs that you have now, or take space away from another room, which will add cost and shouldn't be at the expense of that room if you are keen to add value.

You don't always need the exact same space as you would normally have for a staircase, as there are specialist 'space saver' stairs available. These have a step up on each side of each tread, reducing the space required to fit it in the area, especially from a height perspective. The staircase will need to have a wall up one side, which you might have to add as a partition wall from other rooms.

- **See if you can incorporate windows into the conversion.** The more light you have, the more expensive your conversion will be, but this is one occasion when it should be a major consideration rather than an after thought (see the box, opposite).
- **Think about adding new services or extending your current systems.**

Creating new wiring for electrics/ lighting tends to be fairly easy as most of the wiring is likely to be in the loft anyway, so as long as the current circuit has extra capacity, then this is an easy fix. If you can afford it, go for a new circuit so that existing circuits don't become overloaded. You can also either extend the heating system upstairs, even if it is a radiator, or look at providing independent heating and plumbing so there is less pressure on the current system. In some cases, especially if it's a third or fourth floor that is being created, you may need a macerator toilet in case the waste pipes become too long.

 Many people see a staircase as a small item in the house. However, when you are taking one down, replacing one or putting a new one in, it is subject to stringent building regulations as this is often the only route of escape in case of fire. Without building regulations approval, the loft conversion may be unsafe and will not be signed off by the building inspector.

 For a description of the different types of roof shapes and finishes, see pages 24-5.

Types of loft window

There are lots of different types of window available, which usually dictate what your loft conversion looks like from the outside.

Mansard/mansard roof

This is where additional space is created by part of the new roofline protruding from the existing roof in an 'A' shape. A mansard is mostly used within inner cities where there are quite a few terraced properties and one of the few ways of easily extending is up.

Dormer

A dormer is often seen on chalet properties or some bungalows when there isn't enough height across the whole of the loft area, or you need the height for a shower. A dormer can also help create the height required to put in a staircase and the balustrades that help to ensure the stairwell is protected if someone were to fall.

Rooflights

If you have enough space, then windows flush to the existing roof may be all that is required. They are ideal as they are easy to fit and you often see them on new barn conversions. Velux is a well-known brand.

Other window considerations
- You must be able to open them to clean them.
- The glass needs to be heat reflective so that the conversion doesn't get too hot on a sunny day.
- If the windows are very high up, you must be able to open and close them remotely.

Key steps — Creating a loft conversion

- Work out if your loft can be converted
- See where you can fit in a new staircase
- Get a survey from a member of RICS to confirm feasibility
- Gain planning/building regulations approval
- Lay protective coverings on carpets to ensure builders/contractors coming into your home won't trample in dirt
- Create a dormer, if required
- Create a temporary access to the loft space
- Strengthen the existing floor
- Re-site any existing water tanks/pipes/wiring/telecoms (first fix)
- Insulate the floor area to latest standards
- Put down the new flooring
- Install the chosen windows
- Create the internal space with partitions, if necessary, and boarding up the existing structure to create an internal wall and ensuring they are insulated
- Second fix wiring/plumbing/telecoms
- If not done already, create the new staircase
- Plaster the boarding
- Decorate and furnish
- Get appropriate certificates

Costs

Loft conversions cost anything from around £20,000. Large or more complicated conversions with plumbing for a bathroom can cost up to £50,000. For a DIY fit, the conversion may cost anything from £5,000.

“ A bad job won't add value. Go for professional work that carries a guarantee. **”**

Property tip

Don't forget: a bad job won't add value. So even if it costs a few thousand more to have a professional job done that comes with a valid guarantee, it is worth the expense. Look for companies with the longest guarantee, ten years or more, and always make sure that it is still in force should they go out of business – it may well pay back in the long run.

CREATING A BASEMENT

f you already have a basement, then converting it for use is a fairly simple and cost-effective procedure. If, however, you are creating a basement from scratch, the work will take a lot of time, be very disruptive and cost an enormous amount of money in comparison to other ways of creating extra space described in this chapter.

As a result, if you are thinking about a basement, and one doesn't currently exist, check first the feasibility and costs of creating the space you need elsewhere and only go down this route if it is absolutely what you want or there is little other choice.

Converting a basement

In most cases, you won't require planning to convert an existing basement. To be sure, ring your local planning office, and preferably put something in writing to them so they can confirm that you can go ahead with the work – always a useful document if you sell your property.

Next, measure the current height and width of the room. Ideally, your basement will be 2.4m or more high and the standard tends to be around 2.7m high. As far as width is concerned, there are not really any limits – as long as it's still within your boundary. Most people just convert the space they have, but some go beyond, say into the back garden, which helps create more light for the underground room. Extending beyond the home can have other benefits as you could give a separate entrance from the outside. However, make sure that you have a good security system so you don't make it easy for someone to break in.

The key to a successful basement conversion is the ability to rid the area of damp and, indeed, make it waterproof so it doesn't become a swimming pool during heavy rainfall (see the box, page 154). To do this, you need to ensure that the basement is well ventilated. You must also strictly adhere to the building regulations – especially to make sure that the area is structurally sound. Only a qualified and experienced surveyor can do this for you.

Creating a new basement

This is an enormous task, so make sure you take all the professional advice that you can. You will also need deep pockets, but in some areas of the UK where house prices are high and additional space adds huge amounts of value, you may be able to recoup some, if not all, of the cost.

The key consideration is the type of land that your home is sitting on. For example, if there is a high water table that may cause flooding, the cost of

To find a local qualified surveyor, go to the website for the Royal Institution of Chartered Surveyors: www.rics.org.uk.

preventing this from happening may be out of your reach. Also, if the mains drainage runs underneath your house, it would be an enormous task to try to re-route it. It is likely, too, that this would cause problems not just for you but your neighbour, whose pipes may also be affected.

Once you have checked this out, ensure the foundations are either good enough to cope with the excavation, or (which is more likely) that they can be underpinned for safety's sake. If you are in a terraced property, this is particularly important to understand as you will need a Party Wall Agreement with your neighbours.

Introducing light

If it is impossible to get any natural light in, you may want to have a dark room, cinema room or late night parties! In this case, you will probably want mood lighting rather than bright lights. If, however, you are looking to create a kitchen, extra sitting room or a study, really think through whether you can live without natural light.

If you can't, then a small extension out into the garden area may allow you to add 'light pipes', which are put in the ground (often looking like a small dome shape), and they 'pipe' in the light to the room downstairs.

Another option is a window well, which is basically a double-glazed window that lays flat on the ground and passes light through to the basement. The key benefit of a window well is that it can also improve ventilation. This can be done in similar ways to ventilating a bathroom, such as using humidifying fans or an air pipe. If you can, just putting in windows/doors can help to ventilate the room just like any other in your home.

Damp-proofing your basement

When you come to damp-proof your basement, there are two main methods – make sure that you choose the best for your basement conversion/creation.

Cement-based system This system basically stops any water from entering your basement. It sets a bond with the masonry substrate, creating an impervious barrier to the movement of water.

Water membrane system This is particularly suited to waterproofing old Victorian basements. A membrane is sealed to the walls, ceiling and floor and then covered with plasterboard, screed or a floating timber floor. The difference with this system is that it allows water to drain away, often with the help of a pump and drainage channel.

Property tips

- When looking for someone to convert a basement, look for companies that are recommended by the Basement Information Centre (www.basements.org.uk), which runs Accredited Contractor Schemes, and the Federation of Master Builders (www.fmb.org.uk).
- For underpinning and water-proofing/damp-proofing, there are organisations such as the Association of Specialist Underpinning Contractors (www.asuc.org.uk) and the Structural Waterproofing Group (www.structuralwaterproofing.org).

OTHER CONSIDERATIONS

Think carefully about how you will heat your basement. Ideally, get the cleanest, safest form of heating to help keep you warm. This will invariably be electricity, as any gas services require a flue to discharge emissions. As with loft conversions, it may be best to create a separate ring main for the electricity so you don't overload your existing system.

Finally, think about whether the room would benefit from soundproofing –

❝ Unless you are planning to have a dark room, allowing for natural light into a basement is a key consideration. ❞

Key steps   Converting a basement

- Discuss your plans with an architect and/or surveyor
- Check planning permission and building regulations
- Check if underpinning is required
- Ensure you have a Party Wall Agreement in place, if necessary
- Excavate the area, if you are creating a new basement
- Pump out any existing water
- Do any further excavation/underpinning required
- Create a structurally sound basement
- Apply a liquid damp-proofing
- Damp-proof the floor with a damp-proof membrane

- Create the ground floor structure
- Damp-proof the walls
- Plaster the inside walls with damp-resistant plaster or fix corrugated sheets and then plaster over these
- First fix electrics/plumbing/telecoms
- Soundproof the ceiling, if required
- Restore the original stairs and stairwell
- Second fix electrics/plumbing/telecoms
- Decorate and finish
- Get appropriate certificates and guarantees

especially if it is your teenage kids' room! And if you need the storage, think about how you can incorporate this cleverly within the basement scheme. For example, if you are creating seating, think about being able to store things below, or having some cupboards on the walls to help store what you need, without it looking cluttered.

Costs

Costs vary dramatically, but will always be in the thousands of pounds due to the nature of the job and the time the work takes. Estimates are from £10,000 to £30,000 for a conversion, £40,000 plus for a standard sized new basement through to £100,000 for a large version.

Property tip

The huge benefit of getting a reputable company in – even if it costs you more – is that you get good guarantees with this type of work for ten years, or more. This is worth having as a basement that goes wrong and especially floods, will cost a lot to put right.

Decorating and finishing

There is a big difference between walking into a home that is well decorated and finished inside versus a property that needs a lot of work. That's why people pay a premium for a beautifully finished home. However, be warned that decorating and finishing a property to a high standard takes attention to detail and patience.

Redecorating your home

The first thing to do is to think about what style you want throughout your home. Are you looking for a period theme or would you prefer something ultra-modern? Be warned that styles and trends change very quickly, so if you go for a contemporary look, you may need to change it next year to keep up with fashion – and that can soon add to the cost.

Think through the kind of home that you want to create. Spending money on expensive finishes is nice if you can afford it, but if you have toddlers or teenagers running around the house on a regular basis, you may well end up spending your time worrying about your home rather than enjoying it.

CHOOSING A COLOUR SCHEME

Start by working out what sort of colour scheme you want. Look at what you already have in the room, partly for inspiration and partly to ensure the colours you choose integrate with what you already have. Look around each room and write down the things that you like the colour of – it might be the tiles on a Victorian fireplace, your curtains, bedding, a sofa or lampshade. Mix these ideas with ones you like in magazines and then see what colours work together by working up a colour palette for each room.

The key to good decorating and finishing is to spend time testing different looks, getting samples, and looking at them in different light conditions such as day and night. It is also important to live with the look for a few days to ensure you make the right decision. You can also use online tools (see box, below) to see what your colour scheme would look like.

Wall covering choices

When covering your walls there are a variety of options to choose from. Sometimes the state of the walls will dictate which wall covering you need to have (see the table, opposite). Painting is the easiest option as it can be cleaned and is not difficult to 'freshen up' with another coat. However, you should choose your paint very carefully as the quality can really vary. A good-quality paint will cover the old one with just a few coats. This also has the advantage of bringing out the new colour better than

For help with styles and colour schemes, visit www.dulux.co.uk. www.bbc.co.uk/homes and www.crownpaint.co.uk.

ust putting a few coats of the new one over the original strong colour. Similarly, o enhance the quality of wallpaper, it is always a good idea to use lining paper as t helps the patterned wallpaper on the op to have a better finish.

Tiles are another popular option, but mostly for bathrooms and kitchens. As with wallpaper, it is a good surface covering which, if the wall is straight, can ook good and helps to stop moisture being absorbed into the walls and causing damp. A further option, particularly for bathrooms, are panels that already have a look and feel to them like tiles or a painted surface. These are a new concept but are low maintenance as there is no grouting, the panels have a wipe clean surface and inhibit mould growth (see page 121). Just make sure when you are tiling a wall that this is what you want – paint and wallpaper is not difficult to take off and replace, but tiling is more expensive to fit and remove.

Choices of wall finishes

Type of wall finish	Advantages	Disadvantages
Paint	• Quick to apply • Wipe down to clean • Easy to change the colour/ freshen up	• Doesn't look good on a poor surface • Can require lots of coats if painting over a strong colour • Needs to be applied carefully to avoid drips and uneven application
Wallpaper	• Good covering for blemished walls • Gives a really smooth surface, especially when using lining paper • Excellent variety of finishes/ looks	• Not always easy to wipe clean • If using patterned wallpaper, difficult when the walls aren't straight to get it to match • Sometimes used to cover bad plaster/damp, which might come through later, and then would have to be removed
Ceramic tiles	• Provides a waterproof covering in areas such as showers/ bathrooms/kitchens • Create a bespoke look choosing and mixing different styles • Sturdy covering, which can be easily wiped clean	• If the surfaces aren't prepared properly and waterproof grouting isn't used, tiles will fall off • Messy and expensive to change • Cold to touch and need to be wiped down regularly

Whether you get in a professional or do the work yourself, make sure you don't buy the cheapest products. Opt for the ones that offer a good guarantee, such as lifetime or will last for at least five to ten years.

Flooring choices

Take time to consider what type of flooring you want as there is so much choice and once it is down, it isn't easy to take back up again. If you don't yet have any floor covering and the floors have been newly laid, then you can pretty much choose what type you want. However, as with tiling on walls or hanging wallpaper, if you have old floors that may not be level or ones with dips and bulges in, inflexible flooring, such as laminate and wood flooring is unlikely to be suitable.

If there is already flooring down, check what is underneath. A few lucky people might have some fantastic floorboards or terrific tiles that can be brought back to life. For most of us, though, they are likely to be concrete or plasterboard floors, the latter of which is likely to be fitted to joists.

The main differences between flooring are how they feel underfoot, noise levels and, in some cases, suitability to certain rooms. For example, carpet isn't a great idea for a kitchen! There is also a health reason for choosing some flooring as carpets aren't always best for those with allergies. Carpets can harbour dust mites, which can cause problems for people who suffer from eczema and asthma. The table opposite describes the main things to consider when choosing flooring.

Costs

The costs involved for decorating are lower than most other professions, depending on where you live. An average room that has its walls prepared well and painted should cost around £300, including materials. Covering walls can cost anything from £1.50 per square metre for DIY painting to around £100 per square metre for professional fitting of high quality tiles. On average, budget from £5 per sq m for wall coverings, apart from tiling which will be around £35–£50 per sq m (see also www.designsonproperty.co.uk).

Property tip

If you are keen to get the look of real wood, but can't afford solid wood flooring, investigate 'engineered wood', which is less expensive but has layers of real wood flooring. Always have your home professionally surveyed for real wood as it can expand and contract depending on the humidity and has even been known to push out walls!

For more advice on different flooring materials, go to www.carpetright.co.uk (carpets), www.wickes.co.uk (laminates), www.flooringsuppliers.co.uk (wood), www.carpetright.co.uk and www.diyfixit.co.uk (vinyl and linoleum) and www.tiles.org.uk and www.toppstiles (ceramic and stone tiles).

Choices of flooring

Type of floor	Advantages	Disadvantages
Carpet	• Quick to lay • Covers bumps or dips • Good insulator • Soundproof	• Can attract and retain dust mites • Better to be fitted by a professional • Stains can be difficult to get out and may need professional cleaning • Not ideal for bathrooms/kitchens
Ceramic tiles and stone	• Easy to keep clean • Good for kitchens/bathrooms as waterproof • Hard wearing • Creates a bespoke finish	• Cold underfoot • Requires a level surface • Best to have an expert to fit • Grouting may need cleaning
Laminate	• Can look as good as real wood • Fade resistant • Deals well with spills and accidents • Economical to fit as you only buy what you need	• Can be noisy • Requires some joinery and fitting skills • Can scratch and is difficult to fix • Not any good for floors that aren't level
Vinyl or linoleum	• Good value • Warm underfoot • Durable and waterproof if sealed • Easy to fit	• Can be slippery when wet • Some are poor quality • If not fitted well and sealed, can result in damp beneath the flooring
Wood	• Looks good • Quality wood flooring is very hard wearing • Can add value to a home • Good quality is expensive compared to other flooring	• If original, may be uneven and parts need re-doing • Requires experts to assess suitability and fit the flooring • Needs a flat surface to fit • Not suitable for high moisture areas, such as kitchen and bathrooms

Flooring will cost anything from £5 per sq m for a cheap carpet or laminate DIY job, to £150 per sq m for high quality real wood fitted by an expert. On average, budget around £50 per sq m for flooring within your home.

PROBLEMS THAT CAN ARISE

Particularly in older properties, problems can arise that will affect your finishes.

Damp

Whatever finish you are looking to achieve, making sure you have no timber and damp problems is critical. Ignore the signs and anything you spend will be ultimately ruined. Damp occurs because your home is not waterproof. It may be that the guttering is leaking, causing damp in the roof and down walls. Or it may be that you have damp in the floor or at the bottom of walls. It isn't difficult to detect damp and it is usually easy to fix and fairly economical. To detect it:

- You can often see it, especially rising damp, on plain plaster or in the corner of painted or wallpapered walls.
- Use a damp meter to check if any of the walls or floors are damp.
- Get in a timber and damp specialist, who will usually do a survey for free.

To solve your damp problems, employ a good timber and damp company who will recommend how to permanently fix the problem.

Dry and wet rot

A real silent killer that can affect any finish is anything that rots timber, or creepy crawlies that decide to move in! Dry rot and wet rot are fungi that grow by taking moisture out of your property - especially the timbers, which then dry out. It is one of the worst things that you can get in your home because it can spread everywhere and is a really messy and expensive job to get rid of. Dry rot can be detected by a specialist contractor and it's best to check with a few companies the extent of the problem and what needs to be done to sort it out.

Woodworm

Woodworm make their way into any timber in the home, lay their eggs and disintegrate wood by living and moving within it. In many older homes it is possible that woodworm has got in at some stage and redundant holes may still be visible. Treating exposed timber for woodworm is not difficult and just requires spraying or professionally treating unless the woodworm is in areas of the property that aren't exposed such as an internal beam. If you don't address this before you decorate, it will affect your finishing touches to the point that they may need re-doing.

For more information on dealing with damp and infestation, visit www.property-care.org, www.bricksandbrass.co.uk, and www.petercox.com.

Specialist homes

This chapter gives an insight into the different types of home that you can create to improve your lifestyle. Whether you want to be self-sufficient in a sustainable home, or drain the national power grid with an automated home, this chapter gives you practical guidance, an idea of costs and whether you should do it yourself or leave it to the experts.

10

A sustainable home

Creating sustainable homes for the future is now government policy. In the main, it applies to new homes being built, but if you already have your own home, it is still possible to work towards creating a sustainable home.

SO WHAT IS A SUSTAINABLE HOME?

In its simplest form, a sustainable home is one that doesn't use anything in its build or use that would detrimentally affect the environment for the future. The main culprit for damaging the environment is CO_2 emissions. This is basically a gas that you can't see or smell, and is believed to be the main cause of the climate change we are experiencing today. It is increasingly important that any homeowner becomes aware of the damage their home is causing to the environment, but also does something about it. Furthermore, from August 2007, some homes for sale will require an 'Energy Performance Certificate'. This assesses how well your property uses services to provide energy in the home for heating and hot water.

❝ Homeowners should be aware of any damage their homes do. ❞

WHAT ARE THE BENEFITS?

The main benefit of creating or adapting your home to become more sustainable is that you know you are benefiting the planet – you will also be making a saving on bills. According to recent research that the Energy Savings Trust carried out, buyers are willing to pay up to £10,000 more for an environmentally friendly home. The rationale behind this claim is that people tend to prefer homes that have a boiler that is in good condition and double-glazed windows.

There is lots of information about how to save money, from fitting draught excluders around a doorframe to 'bore holes' in the garden, enabling you to have your own, free, water supply. The savings you can make can vary from a few pounds to over £300 per year, depending on the age and type of home you have. So it is worth exploring what you can and cannot do from a financial perspective.

 To see what an Energy Performance Certificate looks like and the information it contains, visit www.communities.gov.uk and search for Energy Performance Certificate.

Apart from the benefit to your bank balance, there is an enormous upside to the environment that everyone can achieve. According to the World Wildlife Foundation, 'Homes generate nearly 30 per cent of the UK's carbon dioxide emissions', and obviously the more we can reduce this, the better our environment will be.

A home normally feels at its best when it doesn't need any artificial heating, so it feels neither too stuffy nor too cold. So another benefit of creating a sustainable home is that it needs less heating and therefore should provide better air quality.

ADAPTING YOUR HOME

Adapting your home to be more sustainable through energy efficiency can be easily done, much of it without spending any money or taking any time. Other initiatives cost thousands and require substantial changes. Your decision is how much you want to adapt your home to become sustainable.

Once you have adapted to a new way of saving energy and water (see the list, below), there are other areas that you can look to invest in to make your home more sustainable.

Start by filling in the information on the Energy Saving Trust website

Immediate changes that cost very little

- Turn off lights when you leave a room.
- Turn your heating and water thermostats down by 1°C (can cut your bills by 10 per cent).
- Save water. Try not to let water run down the drain – use a plug or bowl in your basin. When you're making a cup of tea, only fill the kettle with the amount of water you need to make it.
- Opt for a shower rather than a bath – you'll use about two-fifths of the water, as long as it's not a power shower.
- Only use the dishwasher, washing machine or tumble drier with full loads.
- Keep appliance temperature settings low and make use of energy or time-saver options if you have them.

- If you have appliances, such as televisions and stereos, that use a similar amount of energy on standby as they do when turning them on, turn them off properly.
- Defrost your fridge and freezer regularly so they run more efficiently.
- Close curtains at dusk to stop heat escaping.
- Move your furniture away from radiators to allow heat to circulate.
- If you're charging something like a mobile or cordless phone, only charge it for as long as is needed.
- Recycle as much as possible, including using bath water (if nothing added) to water your garden.
- Don't leave taps on when cleaning your teeth.

www.energysavingtrust.org.uk on the home energy check page, which gives you a guide as to where you can start to make your home more energy efficient. Ask for the results to be emailed to you, as sometimes the PDF download doesn't work. This will give you your own summary of how efficient your home is and what you can do to improve it.

Insulation

One of the best ways of reducing the amount of energy you use – and therefore making your home more sustainable – is to make sure that when you heat your home, as little as possible is wasted. The following areas are the most likely to lose heat:

- Walls: 35 per cent
- Roof: 25 per cent
- Draughts: 15 per cent
- Floors: up to 15 per cent
- Windows: 10 per cent.

Interestingly, when you compare this heat loss ratio to the cost of reducing it, the most savings can be made with a small amount of money being spent.

- Insulating your wall: £300–£2,000
- Insulating your roof: £150–£300
- Excluding draughts: £40–£100
- Insulating the floor: £200+
- Windows: £2,000–£8,000

So the second cheapest way – insulating your roof – is the most cost effective. To be truly sustainable, use insulation that is naturally produced (recycled paper or

Property tip

Try to find a company that can fit the insulation for you and obtain any grants available. This is often the most economical way of adding insulation. Not only can it be the cheapest, but this is also better than trying to do it yourself. The fibreglass requires you to use a mask and gloves and can irritate the skin. The Energy Savings Trust will offer companies who can do this: www.energysavingstrust.org.uk.

❝ To make your home more sustainable, make sure that your insulation is as effective as possible. ❞

sheeps' wool). However, this can be more expensive than standard insulation made of fibreglass.

Heating

Whether you are heating hot water or using a boiler to heat your home, you can save money by ensuring that any hot water cylinders are lagged in the best insulation jacket you can afford. Any new boilers need to be condensing boilers (see page 113), and these automatically reduce your need for energy as they are more efficient, saving up to 32 per cent on your bills.

Another way to make your home more sustainable is to switch to a 'green' energy supplier, such as www.ecotricity.co.uk or use the Which? website – www.switchwithwhich.co.uk – to help identify other suppliers. This would mean that any electricity you use in your home would come from a sustainable resource, such as wind or tidal power, and therefore reduce carbon emissions. If you have an open fire or any other wood-burning appliance, then another, usually easy to obtain, source of sustainable fuel is wood.

If you really want to ensure that you adapt your home to be more sustainable, you'd need to heat your home and water with sustainable fuel, such as using a special boiler that can be fuelled by 'biomass', which comes in small pellets. For domestic use, these pellets are made from wood, but can be made from other types of vegetation, including sugar cane or even sewage! You would need to buy a special domestic boiler to do this and they can cost five times or more the price of a normal boiler, while saving around £300 a year on fuel bills.

It is only recently that solar and wind technology has been adapted for the home, making it more economically viable. However, be warned that this area has therefore attracted some cowboys who 'over sell' the benefits, in particular of solar power. Before you agree to use any of these new technologies, make sure that the company you are intending to use is a member of the relevant organisation and that you take heed of the suggestions on pages 94–6.

Solar energy

There are three ways of utilising solar energy. Consider these options:

- **Through 'passive' solar heating.** This works in a more sophisticated way than glass in a conservatory. The glass directs the sunlight into the room, but in a format that cannot be passed back through the glass, so becomes trapped in the room. This method is often used in large buildings that have a large glass façade, but you can easily begin to do this in your own home by opening curtains during the day and closing them at night.
- **Through 'solar collectors',** which can help to heat hot water systems. This is done by panels on roofs.
- **Via 'photovoltaics',** which generate electricity from the sun's energy via 'voltaic cells', which are thin layers of semi-conducting material (usually silicon). When this material is exposed to light, an electrical charge is generated, which can then be created as direct current. Lots of these cells are added together to form the solar panels that you see on people's roofs or in their gardens.

❝ The market for new solar and wind technologies has attracted cowboys who over-sell the benefits. ❞

The cost of solar power

A typical solar water heating installation using the flat panels you see on a roof is likely to cost £2,000–£3,000, including installation. A system that uses an evacuated tube collector, which can heat to higher temperatures, costs £3,500–£4,000. Photovoltaics are significantly more expensive and can cost anything from £6,000. If you opt for one that incorporates the solar energy in tiles, the cost increases from £7,500 upwards.

These prices are approximate and will vary based on how many panels you need and other elements of the system you choose.

An average household will save about 50 per cent of the annual cost of providing hot water using solar panels and the same when generating electricity for the home.

Wind power

The Windsave wind turbine is the first small wind turbine that uses wind power to generate a direct supply of electricity compatible with your mains supply. The generated electricity is plugged into your home's standard mains supply via a patented box. The turbine does not operate as a stand-alone system (so you still need mains power – and it won't work if there's a power cut). Instead, it supplements your normal electricity supply and contributes towards reducing electricity bills.

Windsave estimate that the turbine can deliver potential savings of up to 30 per cent of your electricity bill – depending on how much wind you have

The cost of wind power

Installing a wind turbine system doesn't come cheap: from £2,000 to over £6,000. However, a turbine typically comes with a long-term guarantee and can last up to 15–20 years. In terms of payback, the reviews to date are mixed; they can pay for themselves in five years or may take longer. This depends on how much you paid for the system and how much electricity it is generating for your home.

To find our more about installing a solar panel, see www.greenenergy.org.uk. Make sure you use a company that is an accredited installer, who can secure any grants that are available to help with the costs. See www.lowcarbonbuildings.org.uk for more information. For a wind turbine installer, go to www.lowcarbonbuildings.org.uk, who will also be aware of any available grants.

locally. It is therefore important that you position the turbine in the windiest possible position, such as on a gable end or the side wall of a building. Before installing one, it helps to check what the wind speed is like in your area. For the turbine to work, you need speeds of 4–15 metres per second. Visit www.bwea.com to see if your area meets these requirements.

Water resources

Another great way to create a sustainable environment is to reduce the amount of water that you need, or even find your own source. There are various ways to help you conserve water in the home:

- Fit a water butt in the garden – helps reduce the 'new' water required for the garden and washing the car.
- Fix any leaky taps – they can waste over 16 litres of water every day.
- Have showers rather than baths (except that power showers use the same amount of water as a bath).
- Consider having a water meter fitted to help monitor and try to reduce your water usage/bills.
- Use appliances that use less water, such as dual-flush toilets, which when partially flushed use 30 per cent less water than a normal flush.

One dramatic way of reducing your water needs is to provide your own from rainwater. These systems are called 'rain harvesting systems'. They collect water when it rains, on a slightly grander scale than a water butt system. The best place to collect water from is any roof structure, or via your driveway. The water is then taken to a storage tank that is usually placed underground and the water then goes through a filtering process so that it is clean of any debris. Although you can use the water for most things, rainwater harvesting wouldn't normally be at a standard for you to drink.

The cost of a rain harvesting system

On average, these systems cost from £2,500, including the installation costs. Unfortunately, unless installation happens at the start of a build, rather than on a current home, the reasons for installing are more for achieving sustainability than saving money. Larger projects, such as housing developments, industry and agriculture, will have a much shorter payback time and savings could run into many thousands of pounds.

❝Reducing the amount of water you use has great environmenal benefits.❞

The Environment Agency website has lots of information about rain harvesting systems and how you can assess whether or not they are right for you. Visit www.environment-agency.gov.uk.

Boreholes

A fairly new idea for domestic properties is finding your own source of water. Depending on the ground your property is on and what lies beneath, a water borehole could help provide extra water at a time when there is a hosepipe ban. The only downside is that you have to use electricity to run the pump to access the water (although solar panels and wind pumps could do this) and you may need to gain a licence from the Environment Agency to access the water legally.

Products that you can buy

Another way to help create a more sustainable home is to buy more sustainable products to use in your daily life. The list of items that you can buy is huge, but do bear in mind that in most cases the cost of these products is higher than those from less sustainable sources. To easily identify what products you can buy to help make your home more energy efficient, look out for the energy saving recommended logo from the Energy Savings Trust or go to www.energysavingtrust.org.uk.

One easy way to save money and use less electricity is to buy energy efficient light bulbs, which may, at some stage, become the only type of bulb that you can buy. Other sustainable products are energy-efficient appliances, especially those that use less electricity to run, such as tumble dryers, dishwashers and extractor fans. Any solar-power-charged products that don't require electricity are a good way of reducing your dependence on non-sustainable energy resources.

From a home improvement perspective, you can now buy virtually everything you need from sustainable materials. This includes timber from sustainable forests, cleaning products and much more.

" There are many everyday products made from sustainable sources, but they are likely to cost more than traditional products. "

For more information on boreholes and to see if you need a licence or not, visit www.environment-agency.gov.uk or call the Environment Agency on 08708 506506.

Adapting for the disabled

There are various ways that you can adapt your home for yourself or someone who is disabled. In this section we look at various adaptations that can be made to the home for people in a wheelchair, on crutches, with sight or hearing difficulties and for those with dementia or who are unsteady on their feet.

GETTING HELP

Each disability and individual's issues with the home should always be assessed by a professional and this is usually done via a hospital or social services occupational therapist. This is especially required if someone is about to come home from hospital for the first time and they need adaptations, such as grab rails or half steps. If the changes that need to be made are much bigger, it is likely that you will have to wait longer to have them approved and carried out.

There is a lot of help available, from small gadgets that can help someone to be more independent and safe to major adaptations in the home. None of these major adaptations come cheap, so it is important to utilise all the free help you can get initially before you spend your own money. The best place to start is social services, talking to an association that looks after the specific disability that you or the person living with you has, as they are normally the best source of help. If you are not in touch with social services, then you can contact your local council's housing or environmental health department who may have facilities or budgets to help and sometimes they are the route into social services if you haven't already got anyone allocated.

Either social services or your local environmental health department may be able to offer you a disabled facilities grant, which can be up to £25,000 per home for necessary home improvements. They also sometimes offer low-cost loans. However, your income and savings have to be means tested to deem whether you can afford it yourself or not.

Another good route for finding out what help is available is at relevant support groups, which professionals will put you in touch with. These suit some people, but not everyone and they can be a great source of information.

Whatever anyone's disability, here are some simple adaptations that will make a difference:

- **Create the most light you can** – and consistent lighting levels throughout the home.
- **Fit long-lasting bulbs** (such as energy efficient ones) so that they can be changed less often.
- **Decorate with light colours** using a matt rather than a shiny finish.
- **Decorate areas where obstructions or a change in level occur,** to help highlight them.
- **Fit smoke and carbon monoxide detectors,** preferably with alarms or other devices to highlight a problem. The fire service offer a free home safety check and will give free smoke detectors to some clients. Visit www.fire.gov.uk for more information.

ACCESS IN AND OUT OF THE HOME

Most homes have at least one, if not more, steps to get in and out. You'll need to think about access from the front and back of the home and, indeed, in case of an emergency such as a fire.

Try to create either a permanent or portable ramp to the front door. When creating a ramp, make sure it is at the right gradient and not too steep. You will also need to consider resting places on longer ramps for wheelchair users who are self-propelling. Ramps should also have a non-slip surface with a 10cm upstand to all exposed edges to help prevent the wheels going over the edge. For ambulant users of the ramp, handrails can be extremely helpful. The width of the ramp is also an important

Property tip

It is worth thinking about what will happen if you are likely to move at any time. If you are staying where you are, then make the changes you need and with the best material affordable, such as concrete. If, however, you know you will be moving, it could be better to fit wooden ramps that can be easily removed.

 For more information on grants, visit www.direct.gov.uk or contact your local authority.

consideration, especially if a turn is to be included and there must be a 1.2m square landing platform at the top and bottom. A slightly ribbed surface can help people to get up the ramp more easily.

Gradients for a ramp to get over a height less than 2m are recommended to be 1:15 and nothing less than 1:12, even if portable ramps are being used. So if you have a height of 15cm to rise up, you should be considering a ramp that is about 2.25m long. If this isn't possible, you can go less than this if required – but it really depends on the level of disability and how difficult it is to get into the property. If in doubt, get professional advice.

A ramp is also helpful for anyone on crutches, who uses a walking frame, is unstable on their feet or with poor sight or dementia. Of course, they may not need the gradient required for wheelchairs, but taking away the danger of falling is paramount.

" It is important to keep the number of changes in floor level to a minimum, using ramps where necessary. "

MOVING AROUND THE HOME

Once in the home, people should be able to move around easily, such as from room to room as well as upstairs if required/preferred. It is important to reduce the number of floor level changes as much as possible, using ramps where necessary.

For those in a wheelchair, keep corridors free of any clutter and, if possible, allow a clear width of 90cm for people to pass. For those that need help moving around, either provide a walking aid or a grab rail for support on steps or beside a bath/toilet where transfers need to take place. Fit handrails at a height that suits the individual, achieved by an assessment from a professional. These are normally fitted where there are steps, or at convenient places around the home that allow the person to rest as they move around.

If you have stairs and enough space, the best way to adapt the home is to provide everything the person needs downstairs. If this isn't possible, then there are lots of ways of making the stairs safer:

- Add handrails to provide support.
- Ensure the carpets on the stairs are completely secure.
- Check that the lighting is good enough to be able to see each step.

For specific disabilities, such as blindness or Alzheimer's, contact the relevant society. Another excellent site with lots of information and further contacts is www.helptheaged.org.uk.

Alternatively, consider adding a stair lift or even a through floor lift. With stair lifts there are two main types – those you can sit on and those that have a plate for you to stand on. A specialist will come and fit one for you and they cost from £1,500 to buy or you can rent one from £10 a week, plus an installation charge. You can get reconditioned ones for less, but make sure that they have at least a 12-month guarantee and have been reconditioned professionally.

DOORWAYS

For most people in a wheelchair, having a doorway opening rather than a door itself, or at least a sliding door, is easier to manage, as opening doors with handles can be difficult. Doorways need to be at least 75cm wide to allow access via a wheelchair and make sure that any steps within the doorway are minimised. This can be done by using mini ramps so that there is less likelihood of someone tripping over. It is also worth attaching kick plates onto the doorframes so that less damage is caused when the inevitable 'knock' happens.

For someone that is mobile but needs help moving around the home, then it is essential that the doorway is wide enough to get two people through at a time. This may be a standard 75cm width or more, but again get a proper assessment done to see if it's worth widening.

If you are looking after someone with dementia, you need to think about how you can secure – or leave open – doorways. In some circumstances, it may be better to have a lock on doors to rooms that it would be dangerous if they got in, such as a doorway towards a basement. However, it is also important to check doors that are self-shutting or lockable, as these can be confusing for those with dementia. They can get scared and shut in, sometimes trying to find another way out, such as through the window, which can clearly be dangerous. Try to avoid locks on the outside of internal doors as people with dementia can accidentally lock their carer in, which can be disastrous for all concerned.

> **❝Attaching kickplates to doorframes reduces the damage caused by wheelchairs.❞**

Flooring

Different flooring suits those with wheelchairs than those who are a bit wobbly on their feet, for example, so we have suggested the best type of flooring for each disability.

Type of disability	Type of flooring required	Example
Blind	Easy to hear people coming	Well-laid laminate or timber, at a consistent level
Dementia	Pattern free	Carpets, vinyl (all plain), at a consistent level
Hard of hearing/deaf	Ease of cleaning if they have a hearing dog	Vinyl or laminate flooring
Poor mobility on legs	Easy to see, seamless, non-slip	Well-laid laminate, vinyl, carpet
Wheelchair	Easy to use and durable, seamless	Well-laid timber, laminate or vinyl

THE KITCHEN AND BATHROOM

These are two areas that often need the most adaptation but where there are a huge number of ways of doing so. This is to allow people who aren't disabled to live alongside those that are – without inhibiting their independence. For those that are severely disabled, there are many ingenious solutions that can provide great help, so that people can continue to stay in their own home.

The kitchen

First look at reducing the 'danger zone' areas, such as cookers and gas appliances. Then consider height adaptation to some of the kitchen areas so that a wheelchair user or the blind/deaf person can prepare snacks and food for him or herself. From a safety perspective, especially for those who may suffer from dementia or other mental illness, some of the adaptations that are required either prevent accidents happening or give an early warning system when something goes wrong. These adaptations include:

- Keeping the area well lit.
- Unplugging all appliance.s
- Fitting a smoke and carbon monoxide alarm – and testing them weekly (this includes special vibrating pads or flashing lights for those that can't hear).
- Removing any obstacles, such as low coffee tables or rugs.
- Having a fire extinguisher and blanket to hand.
- Keeping any knives or kitchen utensils safely out of the way.

- Installing covers for things like the cooker top, such as a cooker guard
- Positioning a washing machine and dishwasher for easy reach; a top-loading washing machine or tabletop dishwasher might be useful.

If you are adapting your home to share the facilities with someone in a wheelchair or other disabled user, make sure the appliances are more suited to their needs rather than yours. For example, gas hobs can pose a fire risk. Consider cookers that can be left on at little risk and are easy to clean. For example, a halogen hob that isn't hot when touched. Microwaves for those that know they can't put any metal in when heating or defrosting food are also extremely useful and safe options. Built-in ovens at just the right height, with a drop down door that can be used as an extra shelf if required are an excellent way of helping people to be independent, while not impacting on anyone else in the home.

Further adaptations can be made to the physical height of the kitchen to allow wheelchair usage, or indeed restrict the amount of bending down someone has to do, which may be difficult. A guideline for wheelchair users is a worktop at 10cm below the elbow. However, there are many different types of wheelchairs used, so it is best to get the user and the kitchen measured by an expert to know the best dimensions from a height and depth perspective. There are also adjustable height shelves that have their own tabletop cooker, which can be added to allow people of all heights or difficulties to adjust it manually or automatically.

Other considerations are:

- **Corner carousels,** which can be really useful to find things easily.
- **Pull-out worktops,** such as a foldaway ironing board.
- **Mobile trolleys** can provide easy-to-access storage.
- **Easy-to-use handles** – small knobs can cause difficulties.
- **Matt surfaces** to avoid reflective glare, especially for the partially sighted.
- **Position of and type of taps.** They don't have to be at the back of the sink and levers rather than screw taps can be easier to use. There are also taps available for those that have a weak grip or if you need to turn them on and off at floor level. There are even adaptations that can be fitted to your existing taps to make them easier to use.

The bathroom

There are a large number of changes that can be made to a bathroom. The critical elements are to enable anyone, whatever disability they may have, to

 For more information on products that are available for the disabled, go to www.ricability.org.uk, www.epilepsy.org and www.alzscot.org.uk.

adapt the bathroom area to their needs so they can be as independent as possible. For all disabilities, the following checks and adaptations are important:

- Hand-held shower facility
- Grab rails for those moving in a shower or bath
- Non-slip flooring
- An extractor fan to keep the bathroom clear of steam.

Space permitting, you might also want to consider including a hoist to allow someone to be gently lowered into the bath. Alternatively, there are baths available that can be opened and sat in and 'wheel-in showers', which can be specially built to cope with wheelchairs. Some shower cubicles can even be created to cater for both showering and going to the toilet, if they are fitted with a special 'macerator' that gets rid of the waste. This can be particularly helpful in areas where space is tight.

A further requirement is to ensure there is an even temperature of flowing water and that the person using the facilities cannot accidentally scold him or herself, so install a thermostatic or electric shower (see page 123). It is also possible to fix the temperature to a certain range so that no one can be scolded or frozen.

For toilets, it is usually easy to buy adaptations to raise the loo to a required level. This might be just a seat to go on top of the current seat, or some have a frame that can be put over the loo to ensure it is the right height. Raised toilet seats and raised seats with frames are usually readily available free of charge via social services following an occupational therapist assessment.

There are many companies that specialise in fitting these types of bathrooms and you can find them at the www.assist-uk.org website. But before you visit one of the centres, try to get a visit and assessment from your local authority occupational therapist service. They are free of charge and unbiased as they don't benefit from any sales that a company makes, and it's a good way of ensuring you spend your money on what you need, rather than what someone wants to sell you! You can visit and someone will take you around their centre to show you all the different types of bathrooms that can be created. Large companies have a specialist that can come around and assess the best place and type of bathroom fittings that you need. Some will also have showrooms where you can visit and see the facilities in action.

Specialist homes

Some useful websites for bathroom fittings are www.betterlifehealthcare.com, www.carefreebathing.co.uk, www.dlf.org.uk, www.gainsboroughsbd.com and www.ricability.org.uk.

Creating a secure home

According to the Home Office, property crime in England and Wales has fallen by 55 per cent since 1995 and year-by-year burglaries are still dropping. However, there are approximately 733,000 burglaries from the home every year and they account for about 7 per cent of all reported crime. In the main this is attributable to better security features, such as door and window locks and alarm systems.

However, there are still many homeowners that don't provide even the simplest form of security to their home. Although many people think they won't be affected by a burglary, if it does happen, they feel very differently, invaded in some way and have a greater fear of being in the home.

HOW EXPOSED IS YOUR HOME?

What burglars like is a home that people cannot see them breaking into:

- How well lit is the outside of your home?
- Are the lights on all the time, or just when someone is near?
- High walls and hedges give burglars great protection.

They will also use anything you leave out for them to help themselves:

- Are there any ladders lying around that the burglar could use?
- What equipment do you keep in the shed and garage – and what is its value?
- Can the equipment be used to help someone break in?
- How secure is the shed or garage? Is it always kept locked with padlocks and security locks of the highest quality?

What attracts a burglar?

Unlike how we think burglars operate, many of them break in during the afternoon. They spend as little as a few minutes in your home – and still manage to get the things you love and make a huge mess of your home in finding them. Identity theft is very much on the rise, so your personal details are bound to be a main target for them and should be kept somewhere out of the burglar's reach. The following things are likely to attract a potential burglary:

- A spare key that's easily visible, or underneath the plant pot or above the ledge on the door.
- An open window – or windows without any locks.

- A poorly secured door that's easy to take off its hinges or has glass that can easily be taken out.
- Any signs you may be away:
  - No signs someone is in, such as no lighting after dark, curtains always open or closed.
  - Left out newspapers, including the free ones, post or milk bottles.
  - No cars visible when they are normally there.
  - No other signs someone is in such as windows closed when warm.

❝Good home security costs a lot less than the time, money and stress involved in dealing with the consequences of a break-in. ❞

IMPROVING YOUR SECURITY

Every home should have at least the basics of good security. It doesn't cost much compared to the time taken having the police around, tidying up, or re-decorating your home following a break-in. Let alone the time you'll spend justifying what you've lost to the insurance company and then going around replacing it. Here are some cost-effective adaptions:

- **Fit key-operated window locks** to all easy reach windows, such as those at ground floor and off a drainpipe or flat roof.
- **Fit a secondary lock to windows** that open more than 60cm high or wide – such as sash windows or new windows that have a big enough opening for a person to escape during a fire. You can get different types of locks, such as sash stops, which

---

How to check your home's security

Around 20 per cent of homes are broken into via an open window or door and take place, according to West Mercia police, between 1pm and 4pm - in other words, in broad daylight! Ask your local police if they do home visits to advise you on the weak security points. Or ask a specialist security company to visit your home, such as a locksmith and/or alarm specialist with a view to giving you a list of areas where they can improve your security.

For more advice on crime prevention and home security, check out your local police service's website, which is more than likely to contain relevant information.

allow the sash windows to rise only a small distance.

- **If you can, replace glass in easy-to-access windows** with laminated glass, or get a 'film' that can protect your current glass. It's much harder to break and will really put burglars off. Even if they try, they'll find it will just crack, much like a car windscreen, which can be made of similar material.
- **Ensure the doorframes and doors are solid.** Have an external door that is at least 4.4cm thick.
- **Make sure all door locks** are British Standard PAS 24-1 'Doors of Enhanced Security' and all external doors (including ones that open out onto the garden) have five-lever mortise deadlocks (Kitemarked BS3621). These aren't cheap, but are worth it – and your insurance company will expect you to have them fitted.
- **Ideally, for all external doors,** or doors to rooms with expensive equipment, such as an office, dark room or hobby room, look at fitting door security bolts. These bolts go at the top and bottom of the door and have a thick steel or brass bolt that secures the door (or window) more strongly to the frame.
- **Fit a security chain or a door guard,** which is the same thing, but rather than a chain has a fixed steel or brass bar. Make sure you that you keep this on when you are in the home as it prevents the opportunist burglar 'popping' in and taking things quickly when you are upstairs or out the in the garden.
- **A 'viewer'** (which is either integral to the door or something that can be added

later, but use a specialist for a PVC-U door), so you can see who is outside your door can be useful. Keep the chain or door guard on when you open the door and make sure if they claim they are from a legitimate organisation that you ask for their ID. Check it for dates and information and even ring the company (use a number from the phonebook, not on the card) to check they are there for the right reasons.

- **Spread gravel around the outside of the property** – it makes a lot of noise when people walk around and burglars like to be quiet!
- **Fit outside lights** that come on when someone passes, especially against easy entry points, such as front doors. They need to be out of reach of the burglar as best as possible, so fit them over 2m high.
- **Internally, fit intermittent lighting.** This could be timers of which there are sophisticated versions that vary the time they switch on according to the daylight and switch on and off intermittently. There are even ones that allow you to 'phone in' and switch on whatever you have plugged in yourself!
- **Get appliances such as TVs and radios** that have the facility to switch themselves on and off at times you would normally be home.
- **Keep any important documents or valuables in a safe** that is secured to the property in some way – otherwise the burglar will just run off with it! You can also use the look-a-like tins of spaghetti, etc. that are created so you

Average costs of security devices

Depending on the quality you are looking for, the prices given here are the starting point:

Key-operated window locks	£15 for two
Secondary window locks	£15 for two
Glass film	£10 per sq m
Door locks	£25
Door security bolts	£12 for two
Security chain or door guard	£5
Gravel	£10 per sq m
Outside lights	£100 for two
Light timers	£5
Strong padlocks	£30
DIY alarm kits	£100
Installed alarm kits	£1,000, plus £30 per month for monitoring

can keep your valuables in them while you are away.

- Mark all your belongings with something that can be recognised, such as 'smart water'. It takes minutes to do and can cost from £40 upwards, or is free in some areas, depending on local initiatives – ask your local police station what is available. It is especially good for valuables such as pottery and office equipment.
- Put up trellis around fencing so that it is harder for the burglar to get over – especially with roses climbing up.
- Fit strong padlocks to all outside areas such as sheds, and even bars across the windows so that burglars can't get in.

Property tips

- It's easy to go all out to make your home as secure as possible, but make sure that you balance your home's security against the need to escape – or be rescued – from a fire.
- Make sure you create a 'pattern' with your appliances and timer switches. For example, the TV goes off at night when the light and radio goes on upstairs.
- When fitting a lock to a window or door, use the strongest screws you can, not necessarily the ones that are supplied, and make sure they are all to British Standard BS7950. Make sure you also have the keys to the locks hidden away, so you and not the burglar can find them.

BURGLAR ALARMS

Burglar alarms are a great incentive to burglars to stay away. However, some burglars are professional enough to know the difference between a real and 'pretend' alarm and, indeed, some are even able to disable the alarm within minutes.

- **Warning of an intruder.** This could be by an audible alarm that sounds when someone, or something, tries either to break in or to cut the alarm wires. In this case, the police will only attend if someone nearby confirms that someone is trying to break in.
- **Monitored alarms.** These alert the alarm system installer or manufacturer that someone appears to be trying to break in. The installer then rings you or a named neighbour/relative and, if agreed, will then alert the police.
- **CCTV system.** If you have one of these installed, you may even be alerted via a text to your phone that allows you to then check the TV monitor to see what might be triggering the alarm.
- **Infrared monitors.** These can be positioned around the home or in particularly vulnerable areas. They allow you to isolate rooms that you would use at night, for example, while having the alarm set downstairs and in vulnerable areas, such as breaking into an integral garage.

Property tips

- Whichever system you choose, always ensure there is a battery back-up for hard-wired and monitoring systems so the call centre can still be called even if the telephone line is cut.
- If you want the police to respond to your alarm, it must conform to the British Standard 4737 and if a wireless alarm, it must BS 6799 Class VI. Other systems have caused too many false alarm calls. See www.met.police.uk for more information.

 A website that explains how to design and install DIY alarms is www.diy-alarms.co.uk. To search for a professional and for more information, visit www.ssaib.org (the website for the Security Systems and Alarms Inspection Board).

An automated home

It is no surprise that today's technology is cheaper and more accessible than ever. We live with broadband, the internet, cable TV and a multitude of gadgets that are designed to save time and make our lives more comfortable. And, although we haven't quite reached the state where everything is done for us and robots are cleaning the car on a Sunday morning, homes are becoming ever more 'automatic'.

WHAT IS AUTOMATION?

An automated home is already referred to as a 'smart home' or an 'intelligent home'. Although there are many technical definitions of what an automated home is, for the property improver it should just mean utilising technology to help make your home life easier and safer. The types of things that can be classed as automation in a home are:

- Turning lights off and on automatically when it's light or getting dark.
- Opening and closing curtains or blinds remotely.
- Timers that can switch appliances on and off automatically.
- Motorised windows and garage doors that open and close at the flick of a switch.
- Fire and carbon monoxide detectors that can set off sound or flashing alarms.
- Fingerprint recognition door locks.
- Taps that turn themselves on remotely and then off before they overflow a sink or bath.

- Fridges that re-order food when you run out.
- Feeding bowls for pets that open when it's time for tea!
- Robotic vacuum cleaners and lawn mowers.

❝Automation is about making life in the home easier and safer.❞

Home automation installation

There are many companies that promise 'home automation' and also many gadgets being sold for DIY automation. Unfortunately, there is a big difference between a good installation and an effective automation tool. Make sure that any installer has lots of experience of home automation (see box, page 184). It is particularly important they spend as much time asking about what you want to achieve from home automation and how they are going to hide all the wiring, as they do selling you their systems.

ADAPTING YOUR HOME

Adding new gadgets to your home isn't a difficult thing to do. Many of us already have some form of home automation, such as heating controls that switch the heating on and off according to the room temperature and provide hot water. With the growth of broadband, many homes now include wireless technology so that the whole family can connect to the internet from anywhere in the home.

Intelligent systems

However, to truly begin to automate your home, you will need to think about installing an 'intelligent system'. This normally consists of a main hub, which is programmed to suit your requirements. It can be installed to control anything in your home from the lighting to entertainment systems, heating, appliances, and security and safety features. It can also be adapted for remote access away from the home, so you can 'dial' in and request a programme to be recorded or the oven or kettle to switch on so it's ready when you get home.

Depending on your budget, you can have a system like this that controls everything possible or you can have a system for each of the utilities, which you can add to over time. For example, it is possible to have all your lighting automated so that when you arrive home, the drive lights come on, you can then press a remote to open the garage door, which switches another light on. Once you've left your car, the lights show you the way to the front door and by the time you have unlocked it, the lights are switching on as you move from room to room.

Alternatively, you can have your entertainment co-ordinated from around the home. It took years for records to go out of fashion, but it hasn't taken long for CDs to become surplus to requirements. Music and now TV can be downloaded from the internet and played over your computer or media server or sent anywhere around the home or to a hand-held device, such as an MP3 or 4 player. This type of home automation is usually referred to as 'multi-room audio and visual'.

Entertainment systems can also be an automated cinema room with a projector and screen that come down at the touch of a button and lighting and blinds/curtains that adapt to your chosen settings. A more elaborate system can play the same (or different) music/film/TV on monitors and speakers around the home. It can even be programmed to follow you via a detection system which notices when you move from room to room.

 When looking for a specialist, make sure you choose someone from www.cedia.co.uk (the Custom Electronic and Design Installation Association) as they strive to find you qualified, reputable and insured design and installation contractors.

Remote home automation

If you have a second home, or are away from your home a lot, it may be worth considering improving your home to increase security, ensure your garden is always well watered and that if frost is about to hit, you can turn on the heating to ensure that pipes don't burst.

Such technology is made possible by installing software on your mobile phone to access appliances in the home. From a security perspective this can be an excellent facility. If you have a security system that alerts you to someone ringing the doorbell or appearing to try to get into your home (see page 182), you can tune into the security camera and see what's happening. You then know whether to alert the police or if it's simply a false alarm.

Alternatively you can access your control systems from the internet, just as you may access your emails or files from any computer with internet access.

Typically, there is a website that is provided with the networking software you have installed in your home that allows you to access the control system.

Home automation for the elderly and disabled

Both networking and remote systems can be incredibly helpful for those who suffer with any disability. They can save accidents happening, give enormous independence to those who are in a wheelchair, hard of hearing, blind or have mild dementia. It can also allow an elderly relative to live in their own home more safely with devices that can warn them, or you, when something goes wrong.

For those that find it difficult to reach windows or open doors, motorised systems can do the job at the touch of a button. Kitchen units can be lowered or increased in height so that anyone can make their own snack, meal or drink. For anyone who can be easily distracted and needs a reminder to take tablets, switch off the cooker or a tap, devices are now readily available that can sound an alarm or portray a flashing light if someone is hard of hearing to alert the danger. Remote systems can alert a neighbour or relative via a mobile text message.

Costs

There is a huge variety of systems, some which can take a few hours to install, such as wireless networking around the home and cost around £100. A major installation including system design, cable installation, commissioning and programming can take up to six months from start to finish to install and there is no maximum cost. A large-scale installation could cost in excess of £150,000!

Doing-it-yourself

If you are looking at basic home automation, such as creating a wireless network, and have some IT knowledge, there are plenty of kits available to help you set up a broadband wireless connection. There are also some basic networking kits available to help you create basic home automation, such as turning lights on and off via timers. Gadgets that can be bought are usually relatively easy to integrate with any software that you have, but beware that there are some bugs that can happen and having good telephone back-up is essential.

Outside your property

Improving the area outside your property can have a major impact on its value, and on how much you enjoy living in it. A garden that suits your needs undoubtedly improves your quality of life, as does easy access and parking. And the outside is what you, and your visitors, see first when they reach your home, creating an instant impression for potential buyers.

11

Garden boundaries

Before you make any changes to a garden, you want to be very clear on what you own and what you are responsible for. This sounds easy but frequently it isn't: neighbours often don't know, or are wrong, about who owns or is expected to maintain a fence or wall, and disputes about the issue are, sadly, common.

It is particularly important to check on the boundaries of new properties, on those where extra land has been purchased – perhaps to allow for an extension – and any property that has had an altered use, such as a large house that has been turned into flats.
Neighbours may not necessarily be aware if or how a boundary has been changed. One point that won't change, however, is that the local council owns the pavement and highway.

The first port of call is either the drawings of a new property and its boundary, which should have the exact measurements, or look at your title register and title plan (often known as the title deeds), the legal documents outlining who owns what. The solicitor or conveyancer who dealt with the purchase should be able to supply both of these. If they can't, you can buy a copy of any title plan for £6 from HM Land Registry. These plans should help to clarify the position, but the Land Registry plans are fairly small scale and only really show the 'shape' rather than the measurements and so do not guarantee an accurate answer.

Another port of call that may also be worth contacting is your local council as they may have original drawings when any planning permission was applied for. These are usually more detailed and include measurements. If they can't supply the plans, they may be able to tell you who the architect was who may, in turn, find the person who made the

❝ Always check on boundaries of new properties or where extra land has been purchased, as not everyone may be aware of them. ❞

 Copy title plans are obtained via form OC1 from www.landreg.gov.uk, which will also tell you which office to send the form to. Other useful sites for information on boundary law are: www.gardenlaw.co.uk and www.boundary-problems.co.uk.

changes and again be able to provide the original drawings.

If you are lucky, there will be marks in the shape of a letter 'T' on the map. Whoever's property they point towards owns the nearest boundary to the symbol. A double 'T' means responsibility is shared. However, this information is not always recorded.

TALK IS CHEAP (AND LITIGATION ISN'T)

The next step is to talk to your neighbours. They may have information about boundaries in their registry documents or from past practice. Friendly negotiation is the key here: if relations are poor you may have to resort to the legal process. It is also worth pointing out that there is no government organisation responsible for defining private land, so the legal argument can become very complex and last a long time. You could end up spending tens of thousands of pounds on resolving a dispute about land that is worth a fraction of your costs.

Furthermore, amicable relations with neighbours add to your quality of life: you don't want your garden idyll to feel like a war zone. If you don't agree on who owns what or who should be re-building that crumbling wall, discuss it as politely as you can until you reach some kind of compromise. In the worst scenario, you are probably better off just paying for the necessary repairs rather than arguing over a pile of rubble.

WHAT IF YOU WANT TO BUY NEIGHBOURING LAND?

You may decide that one way to improve the value of your property is to increase the amount of land it covers. If there is suitable land adjoining your property, you may have to pay a premium for it because it will be of such a benefit. If the plot is large, buying it could prevent unwanted development, such as building another property close to yours. In England, Wales and Ireland it is possible to claim ownership of land if you have been in effective possession of it for ten years (registered land) or 12 years (unregistered land). If you think this applies to you, take legal advice. Contact HM Land Registry if you don't know who owns the land.

> **❝ No government organisation defines private land, so legal argument can be complex, time-consuming and expensive. ❞**

 Websites giving guidance on garden-related issues include: www.boundary-problems.co.uk, www.gardenlaw.co.uk, www.britishlaw.org.uk and the Land Registry site on www.landreg.gov.uk.

Landscaping your garden

Many people value the design and condition of their garden as highly as that of their home. There is no doubt that an attractive garden helps to sell property, and, more importantly, improves the quality of life for its inhabitants.

Estimates of the material value of a really well-planned garden vary, but some estate agents put it as high as adding 15 per cent to the value of a property. In other words, a decent garden could add £7,500 to the price of a typical home.

Attractive gardens can also encourage viewings and create an excellent first impression. If you are looking to sell a property with a reasonable kitchen and a large but neglected garden, you might be better off investing money in garden design to bring it up to the standard of the rest of the property rather than over investing on the interior.

Expectations of what a garden can do for us have been raised by the plethora of TV makeover programmes and garden shows. Other factors include reluctance to let children play away from home, a trend towards outdoor entertaining (accelerated by the rising availability of outdoor heating and lighting) and a revived interest in growing our own food.

PRIORITIES

Step one in deciding how to make your garden work better for you is to agree what your priorities are (see table, opposite) and how they can be met. Bear in mind that priorities can change – on retirement, perhaps – and sometimes there are good alternatives: for example, children grow out of the need for a play area and maybe the local park is just as good. The more of these priorities (and any others of your own) you can meet, the greater the improvement to your property and your life.

> **❝ Investing in an attractive garden can encourage property viewings and help to create an excellent first impression. ❞**

 Websites to look at to find out more include www.landscaper.org.uk (Association of Professional Landscapers), www.landscapeinstitute.org (Landscape Institute) and www.bali.co.uk (British Association of Landscape Industries).

Your personal requirements

Priority	Requirement
Children	Safety, lawn, Wendy house, tree house
Easy maintenance	Gravel paths, patio or decking
Entertaining	Patio with space for table and chairs, outdoor lighting and possibly heating, barbecue
Home-grown food	Fruit and vegetable patch, compost bin, fruit trees or bushes
Love of gardening	Variety of planting in numerous beds
Pets	Good fencing to keep dogs in, space for kennels/hutches
Privacy	Screening from neighbours
View from house	Careful landscaping
Wildlife	Welcoming habitat, trees and/or bird tables

Kids R us

Children need space, and for many a hard-wearing lawn is a must for ball games. Depending on how much room and enthusiasm you or they have, you might consider play equipment, such as swings, a slide, a climbing frame and a trampoline, while younger children love a sandpit (cover this to avoid 'toilet' issues with the local wildlife). Avoid delicate borders that will suffer under an onslaught of balls and straying legs. If young children are involved, cover and fence any ponds to prevent them falling in. Older children may relish the idea of a hot tub – although your neighbours might not thank you for it if they can hear the noises of the motor and party animals.

Easy maintenance

This is high priority for many who lead the 'money rich, time poor' lifestyle. A lawn is out (unless you employ someone else to cut it) and the emphasis is on 'hard landscaping', such as decking or a patio. Avoid beds and borders and definitely steer clear of pots, which are very high maintenance. Instead, plant weed-deterring groundcover plus shrubs and climbers, and put down mulch between plants to stop weeds growing and keep the soil wet – even better, lay heavy-duty plastic sheeting before adding the mulch. The other option is to pay someone else to do the spadework – worth it if you enjoy viewing the results of their labours.

Entertaining

The idea of the garden as an extra room has caught on big time. For dining, you need an area at least 3.5sq m to fit a table and chairs for a minimum of four people. This should be near the house or the barbecue for ease of access and hassle-free serving and clearing up. A stone patio (less slippery than decking) is far more suitable than a lawn for entertaining. You may want to consider additional lighting to maximise your evening usage, and (if you think the planet can handle it) outdoor heating. A water feature is another possibility as sipping an evening tipple is even more pleasant accompanied by the sound of bubbling water.

Plot to plate

Enthusiasm for home-grown food is at an all-time high, and growing it is so much more convenient in the garden than at an allotment. An easy starting point is growing herbs, which can be done inside as well as out. A dedicated vegetable patch, perhaps in raised beds to ease the strain on your back, is very appealing to anyone with an interest in cooking and organic food. You could also grow fruit on bushes or, if space allows, in your own mini orchard. Running your own miniature farm is demanding work, however, and there are occasional gluts of produce that may have the family

reaching for the fast food menu rather than face another courgette feast.

Love gardening?

If you're the green-fingered type, gardening can be heaven. Top priority goes to beds, borders and planning for year-round colour. You want good soil (see page 195), at least one outdoor tap, a shed and a greenhouse or conservatory. If space is limited, containers give you more to work with.

Pets

Pets aren't usually good for gardens because they mess it up in all sorts of ways. The priority with a dog is sound fencing so the animal can't escape. If smaller livestock, such as rabbits or guinea pigs, are your thing, they'll save you mowing some of the lawn, but leave it nibbled to the bare soil unless you are very good about moving the run regularly. If you're looking to sell the property, make sure that you get rid of any mess and smells that might be lingering.

Privacy

If the garden is overlooked, you can screen it for privacy either with high fencing or evergreen shrubs. However, there are restrictions on the height of these (see page 55) and if you want to build higher, then you will have to apply for planning permission. If noise is an

 Well-qualified garden designers are likely to belong to the Society of Garden Designers (www.sgd.org.uk) and see also the Royal Horticultural Society website on www.rhs.org.uk.

ssue, shrubs will absorb some sound and
will provide a friendly rustle, and maybe
wind chimes or a water feature will block
out some of the intrusion. Sometimes
the intrusion is the smell and sight of a
neighbour's oil tank or bins: you can
remedy this quickly by buying ready-
grown laurel hedging.

Enhancing views

Make the most of attractive views, such as
church towers, thatched roofs and pretty
trees, by framing them with your own
planting. Blur boundaries by allowing your
neighbour's plants to spill over walls or
fences. Add a focal point, such as a water
feature or statue, and divert paths so that
the eye and the body are drawn around
the garden, which makes it seem bigger.

Wildlife

Use native plants and aim to provide
food for local wildlife, such as nuts and

Trunk call

Trees add height to a garden, but
beware of small gardens with mature
trees because they tend to dominate.
Roots of trees planted too near a house
can cause structural problems. Check if
any trees you plan to cut down are
protected (as part of a conservation
area or by a Tree Preservation Order)
by contacting your local planning
authority. If they are, you need to apply
for permission to remove them or to do
any tree surgery, and you may be
required to plant replacements of the
same species and in the same location.

---

berreies, and also breeding areas through
trees that offer nesting sites. Other
elements include a pond, wildflower
meadow and use of stepping stones
to maximise growing space.

The good, the bad and the ugly: turn-ons and turn-offs in the garden

Popular	Unpopular
• Well-maintained appearance	• Trees near houses: roots can cause structural problems
• A healthy lawn	• Large expanses of gravel (giant cat litter)
• Roses	• Poor quality subsoil
• Fruit trees	• Decking that has become green and slippery
• Ponds and small water features	• Ugly walls
• Exterior lighting	• Large water features that are hard to maintain
• Stone patio or well-kept decking	• Traditional conifers (they soak up light and dominate the view)
• Year-round interest	• Swimming pools (high maintenance and take up a lot of space)
• Mature shrubbery	
• Extra colour from plants in pots	
• Slate paths, or slate crushed into mulch	

PLANNING YOUR GARDEN

Once you've set your priorities, either for your needs or as a seller, consider what you can and can't change. This will help you decide on a garden style that is right for you and your property.

Compass points

The garden's aspect is a big influence on how it can be improved: where it is in relation to the sun affects how pleasant it is to relax in and the type of plants that will thrive.

- **North-facing** These get less light, so keep the plan open, avoiding overhanging trees and narrow paths. Plant growth will be slowed by cooler soil. Good for a cottage garden and for creating shady woodlands. Bad for decking, which can easily turn green and slippery.
- **East-facing** These gardens get the sun in the morning – lovely for breakfast on a patio, but not good for evening light or watching the sunset. Keep the eastern and southern boundaries as low as possible to maximise the amount of light arriving. The morning blast of sun can damage early flowering plants because they get scorched, inhibiting growth and pollination.
- **South-facing** The most desirable orientation for the green-fingered as the garden will be in the sun for most of the day, so the air and soil will be warmer, providing excellent growing conditions. Mediterranean sun-loving planting, such as lavender and herbs, should do well. You'll need to plan in some shade from trees, tall plants or grass, or perhaps a pergola.
- **West-facing** Great for evening sun, so the best orientation for a garden that will be used for entertaining. Mornings can be quite chilly, so frosts can be very harsh.

❝ The garden's position in relation to the sun is a key factor. ❞

Adapting your garden

When changing your existing garden, consider these factors first.

What can't you change?
- Boundaries
- Aspect (e.g. north-facing)
- Frost pockets
- Soil type (although you can improve its consistency)
- Slopes (unless you opt for expensive terracing)

What can you improve?
- Screening for privacy and windbreaks
- The proportion of light and shade
- Hard landscaping, such as patios, decking, walls, paths, fencing and pergolas
- The planting
- Adding top soil

Other factors

The soil type and quality has a big impact on what will grow well. Look at what is flourishing in neighbouring gardens and use this as a guide, because the soil type is likely to be the same. The main soil types (which will be present in varying proportions in your garden) are:

- **Clay** Heavy, lumpy and slow to drain. Needs regular digging to allow nutrients to circulate.
- **Chalky** Light-coloured, alkaline soil with many small stones. Needs plenty of fertiliser.
  Loamy A crumbly textured blend of sand, silt and clay, considered ideal for growing.
- **Peaty** High in organic matter, but low in other nutrients. Allows for good growth if drainage is OK.
- **Sandy** Gritty soil that can dry out too quickly, but is easy to cultivate.
- **Silty** Very fertile and easy to work.

Dedicated gardeners will test the pH level and set up an improvement/maintenance process, such as a compost heap and supply of manure and fertiliser. New-build sites sometimes suffer from very poor soil as it has been compacted by machinery and can be polluted by previous industrial use or by dumping of building detritus. If topsoil has been added, it may be full of weed seeds from its previous location, or less fertile subsoil that won't give your garden a chance to develop. So the best way to tackle this is to lay a new lawn (see box, right) and bring in your own top soil.

Wind direction and funnelling is another issue, as wind dries out soil and foliage, and influences where insects grow (and therefore what gets pollinated). Salt-laden coastal winds are particularly damaging to some plants. A living or artificial windbreak will help as will careful location of infrastructure, such as sheds and greenhouses: if they are close to each other, the wind will funnel between them.

“ Soil type and wind direction are two other important factors to consider when choosing plants. ”

Key steps — Laying a lawn

- **Remove lumps and bumps and dig over the soil to create a smooth, level surface**
- **Sprinkle on some granular fertiliser, rake and water**
- **Lay the first row of turf, butting up each one closely**
- **Continue laying in a running brickwork pattern so that joins are staggered**
- **Lay over the edge for easy trimming**
- **Water thoroughly**

GARDEN STYLES

It is important to remember that your garden is part of a landscape, and should reflect the local environment (including your house) as much as possible, otherwise it will look odd. For example, for a stone wall or patio, try to use local stone or the same material that your house is built in.

The choice of garden style is obviously down to your personal preference, but if you are thinking of selling the property, avoid a strongly individual look like a formal Japanese garden as this will limit your market. Remember also that gardens evolve and will change with time, so it is important to plan ahead for the look you want – although you can get a lot done in one concerted burst of activity.

> **❝** If you are thinking of selling the property, avoid a strongly individual look as it could put off some buyers and limit your market. **❞**

Formal or informal?

Your design is likely to fall into either of these categories. Formal gardens are based on symmetry, with a central line of symmetry down the garden and sometimes another line going across, creating four quarters. This is a more traditional look with a strong sense of

Jargon buster

Obelisk A tall, thin, four-sided structure in wood or metal, used either for planting or for ornament

Parterre A formally patterned flower garden, usually square or rectangular

pH level A measure showing the type of soil you have, such as neutral, acidic or alkaline, which helps you to understand what plants will and won't grow in your garden

order and examples of formal garden styles are the Japanese minimalist design or a formal parterre.

The informal style plays with shape to create a more natural look with plenty of curves. Balance is achieved with asymmetry, for example, by having similar shapes or blocks of colour at diagonally opposite points in the garden. Cottage gardens and wildflower meadows are generally informal, too.

Planning and planting

Once you have designed the overall shape, plot what you will plant in the borders. In addition to considering soil, light and shade conditions, plan what colours you want and where. Consider also the height and shape of the plant(s) together with their leaf shape. Planting three plants in a triangle will form a clump over time, which is more attractive than an isolated plant.

Non-plant elements of garden design

It is worth considering these points at the design stage. Do you want them, where will they go? You'll probably need to put them in or at least plan for them before other landscaping and planting work.

Compost bin Valuable for recycling waste and fertilising soil

Electricity You may want it for a pond pump or lighting

Fencing Should last for 20-25 years, but may need replacing sooner

Furniture Consider its style and where it will be stored. If it can't be left out in the winter, where will it go and does it fit?

Hanging baskets Beautiful when planted out, but need lots of watering

Irrigation What will need watering? The minimum requirement is an outside tap. For large gardens, it may be worth considering an automatic watering system

Ornaments Can be artistic, like a statue, or functional, like an obelisk

Paths Not just for access, but to define sections of the garden

Patio Stone looks great if it matches local materials or the house; wooden decking can be stylish and is cheaper, but can become slippery

Pergola, arches and tunnels Bring height and a chance to add interest and a position for climbing plants

Pots and containers Great for adding colour to small spaces and for softening the hard lines of a patio; pots on either side of the front entrance add grandeur

Shed A must for most gardens

Summer house Great for outdoor entertaining, especially if you don't want a patio

Costs

These costs are for general guidance, as so much depends on the choices you make.

Project	Cost	Notes
Seeding a lawn	£1-£2 per sq m	Lawn needs careful preparation
Turfing a lawn	£3-6 per sq m	Instant result, needs preparation and maintenance
Decking	£50-£100 per sq m	
Fencing	£40-£80 per sq m	
Pond	£150-£500	Plus materials
Water feature	£50-£400	Including pump, plus installation costs
Pergola kit, simple arch	£100	Plus labour
Large pergola kit	£300-£500	Plus labour

DO YOU NEED A GARDEN DESIGNER?

Many people enjoy gardening and have a clear idea of how they see their garden developing, backed up with a good understanding of soil, plant types and planting. Many others do not have this knowledge and if you want to improve your garden, particularly if you are in a hurry, it may well be worth employing an expert. A good garden designer will be able to:

- Survey the garden, including analysing the soil.
- Offer a variety of ways of meeting your brief.
- Produce annotated drawings and perspectives of the agreed design.
- Create a full planting plan.
- Provide a full maintenance schedule, including how to care for individual plants.
- Carry out work or help you select a contractor.

Costs

You may just need some of this range of services. Some designers will hold an initial meeting for free; others are likely to charge between £40 and £60 per hour. Agree this in advance and consign anyone who asks for money upfront to the compost bin. Commissioning a border design might cost around £200, while drawings for a complete garden scheme should cost about £500–£600; with a structural and planting plan costing double that. A professionally designed and contracted garden is unlikely to cost less than £5,000 – and many will cost far more than this. Some designers charge a percentage of the whole budget. If this seems high compared to TV garden makeovers, bear in mind that their projects rarely include the cost of labour in their budgets.

Property tips

- **Plan your work so that it is done from the back to the front of the house: there is no point creating a beautifully landscaped entrance to your home if contactors are going to have to cross it to transform the garden at the back.**
- **Plants can be bought very cheaply, but it pays to go to a specialist supplier who has given them a good start. Superstore plants don't necessarily get the love and attention that nursery outlets are geared up to offer so check their condition and compare to your local garden centre or plant supplier before you buy.**

 For information on finding a garden designer and how to employ a contractor, see pages 93 and 94-102.

Driveways & garages

Off-road parking is a major benefit as our roads become more and more congested, and properties that offer it usually get a rise in value.

You want your driveway to look good because it marks the entrance to your property, but it also has to be able to bear the weight of cars and delivery vehicles, and cope with the considerable stresses of power-steered wheels being turned on the spot, grinding a weight of a ton or more into the surface.

Cracks and blemishes in the surface will grow in the winter months when they fill with water, which freezes and expands. Patched up repairs on driveways don't tend to last long because they don't deal with the cause of the problem, which is likely to be poor or worn-out base material. You can have a new driveway laid in a matter of days.

> **Patched up driveway repairs don't last long because they don't deal with the cause of the problem, most likely the base material.**

IMPROVING YOUR DRIVEWAY

Your choice is tarmac, paving or gravel:

- **Tarmac** is used for roads and pavements and is available in black or red. It is the cheapest material (and sometimes looks it) unless the area is quite small.
- **Paving is usually with cubes or flagstones.** Cubes (also known as setts) are blocks of natural stone in a wide range of colours and are extremely durable. Flagstones are flat natural slabs of stone (usually slate, granite or sandstone).
- **Gravel** is the cheapest option and is fine for driveways provided the drainage is good, but it is a noisy surface and can become the local cat litter.

Where and how big?

Houses look better without cars in front of them so, if possible, plan the parking space next to or behind the property. It should be wide enough to easily accommodate a large car, which will be approximately 2.7m wide, and obviously double that for two cars. It should also be able to go back by 5.5m away from the public highway to ensure that the cars are completely off the road. Any curves should be at least one-third wider than the car to allow for turning.

Hiring a contractor

Laying a driveway calls for specialist equipment such as compactors and rollers, and a lot of muscle power. There are many companies that will try to get your business – often from door knocking – and it is extremely important not only to have an independent check from an expert (see www.pavingexpert.com), but it is also worth getting three quotes so that you can see the difference and make sure you are comparing like with like. If you do use a company, make sure that you are around to see the work taking place and that they adhere to the contract of works that they have given you.

> **❝ Laying a driveway requires specialist equipment and plenty of muscle power: go for a contractor. ❞**

Key steps **Making a driveway**

- Check what utilities might be buried under the driveway, such as water

- Excavate the ground to around 20cm below the finished level

- Remove anything that might grow back through, for example, a tree stump or shrub

- Create any drainage requirements

- Compact the base

- Lay any drainage (particularly for concrete driveways)

- Lay any edgings you might have chosen

- Lay and compact the sub-base (mix of small stone and sand)

- Lay and roll flat a base course, often sand

- Add the driveway finish, such as tarmac (wearing course), blocks or concrete

---

For more information on laying driveways and finding an expert, visit www.paving.org.uk (the Precast Concrete Paving and Kerb Association), www.interlay.org.uk (the Block Paving Association) or www.fmb.org.uk (the Federation of Master Builders). Other recommended sites are www.pavingexpert.com, www.drivesbydesign.com and www.diydoctor.org.uk.

Typical costs for driveways

Top layer	Materials (per sq m)	Likely total cost including labour (per sq m)
Tarmac	£30–£40	£60–£70
Concrete blocks	£40–£50	£70–£80
Pavers	£40–£55	£70–£80
Gravel	£30–£40	£50–£60

Costs

The cost of a driveway should include the surface blocks or bricks, plus sub-base material, bedding sand, the dry sand for jointing, skips to remove excavated material and, of course, labour. In the case of tarmac, this is likely to be a four-person team of rake-hand, roller driver and two labourers, charged at £60–£120 per hour. Materials will be an additional cost and these are highlighted on a per square metre basis in the box above.

66 People prefer properties with a garage, even though the days when they were used for cars are long gone. 99

GARAGES

Gone are days when garages were used for cars. However, people still prefer properties with a garage and they can add anything from a few per cent or more to a property, depending on how much parking is at a premium. The highest return being in London where off-street parking and especially a garage could add tens of thousands of pounds to your home.

When choosing a garage, consider the following:

- **The look and feel of your property.**
  If you have a beautiful thatched home and add a 1960s concrete pre-fabricated to it, then you are likely to take thousands of pounds off its value. However, add a mini version of your home, such as an oak-framed garage or a timber motor home, or even one with a thatched roof, and you will add much more than money, your home will look great too! If you have a home with a pitched roof, check to see whether it would damage the look of

the property if you have a garage with a flat roof.

- **Why do want a garage?** Is it for your beloved car or just for extra storage, or to increase the value of your home, or indeed a mixture?
- **If you intend to use the garage for storing your car, what size is it?** Make sure that you know its length and width and, with the ownership of 4x4s, the height of the car, too. In addition, check out how high and wide the boot and passenger doors open. This will make sure you can get in and out easily and, if required, have enough room left over for storage.
- **What, if any, maintenance you are happy to undertake.** For example, if you are looking at a timber garage, you may need to ensure the wood is preserved every few years, whereas

---

Property tip

Don't forget that you may need planning permission for your garage (see pages 53-65). It may be even worth applying for two-storey planning permission and building your garage with strong enough foundations to ensure that you can build on top if you want to.

---

with brick, you'd just need to make sure the guttering is kept clear and in good working order.

- **Your budget,** which will have a big influence on what you can or can't have. Work out how much you would ideally like to spend and how much you would be willing to spend for something really special, such as an oak-framed garage.

Finding the right garage

There are many different types of garages you can choose from, but only really three ways of creating a garage that would be right for your home:

- **Buy a garage that comes flat packed** – a bit like a shed! There is a vast range of garages that you can get in kit form, including timber and concrete, which you can resource online or from DIY stores or places that sell outbuildings, such as garden centres. If possible, visit the showroom and if the company is really helpful, they will allow you to test parking your car in them to make sure they fit and help you size the garage you want.
- **Use an off-the-shelf garage plan** that your local architect might have to hand or you can get online. Such plans can also be provided by

 To see lots of garage plans, visit www.garageplans.co.uk and www.carryduffdesigns.co.uk.

companies that sell standard or bespoke garages. This would allow you to specify the type and size of garage you want. It is a good idea to show the person drawing up the plans a picture of your home so that he or she can help choose a plan that will maximise the look of your property.

- **Create a bespoke plan** using a local architect to ensure that the new building is in keeping with your home and created to your exact specifications.

 As with having a driveway made, building a garage is an area notorious for attracting cowboys. Follow all the checks advised on pages 94–6 before employing someone to do your building work.

Costs

The price, of course, depends on many variables, but on average a concrete base for a single garage would cost around £500–£1,000 (depending on foundations required) and concrete kits can cost anything from just over £1,000 to £5,000 plus.

Oak-framed garages, which are a better material for double garages, are more likely to cost from around £6,000 to £12,000, with larger, more complicated builds costing double this amount. Erection costs will depend on where you live and the supply of labour, but you are likely to be looking at a minimum of £1,500, which would increase dramatically for a large build that is finished to high standard from start to finish.

❝There are three ways to create a garage: buy one flat-packed, use an off-the-shelf plan, or have a bespoke design drawn up by an architect.❞

Building timescales

This chart gives guideline timescales for how long projects can take. As every project is different, some may take less time, others more, but these are average guidelines. Always ask your contractor the likely timescale of a project – and check that they will be on site all the time, rather than come back and do it 'when they can', fitting it around other jobs, as this will inevitably take much longer.

	Timescale
Electrics and plumbing	
Replacing radiators and pipework	5 days+
Refurbishing a heating system	2 days
Kitchen and bathroom	
Removing an existing kitchen	2 days
Fitting a kitchen	1–5 days
Fitting a bespoke kitchen	3–6 weeks
Removing an existing bathroom	1 day
Remodelling a bathroom	1–2 days
Fitting a bathroom	1–2 weeks
Windows and doors	
Buying and fitting a door (self)	1 day
Ordering and fitting a door (joiner)	1–2 weeks
Windows (standard), ordering to fitting	2–4 weeks
Windows (bespoke), ordering to fitting	2 months

“ These timescales can only ever be average lengths of time. So much depends on external events. Nevertheless, they provide a good starting point. **”**

	Timescale
Extensions	
Building an extension (depending on size and design)	4 weeks–6 months
Converting a garage	4 weeks+
Building a conservatory	2–8 weeks
Converting a loft	4 weeks–3 months
Converting or creating a basement	1–6 months
Decorating	
Decorating the walls (including preparation)	1–3 days
Laying a floor (including preparation)	2–4 days
Specialist homes	
Automated home	3 hours–6 months!
Outside your property	
Improving a driveway	2–5 days
Building a garage	3 days–2 weeks

Glossary

APR: Annualised percentage rate.

Attic trusses: Special roof supports that lend themselves to creating a room in the roof.

Balance outstanding: The amount of a loan still owed.

Base rate: Interest rate set by the Bank of England, which is the rate at which banks can borrow money from the Bank of England and therefore the level that the banks use to set their interest rates.

Building inspector: Officer that inspects and signs off building works.

Building regulations: Standards of build set for new buildings, extensions and renovations.

Buildings insurance: The insurance on the structure of a property.

BBR: Bank of England base rate.

Capital: The initial mortgage loan.

CH: Central heating.

Contract: The agreement to sell or purchase.

Carcass: The structure of a kitchen cupboard, behind the door.

Cavity: The space between a double skin wall.

CCTV system: One or a series of cameras that video what is happening in vulnerable areas around the home, such as the front and back door or a conservatory.

City and Guilds: A training organisation that awards vocational qualifications.

Contingency: An amount of money over and above the budget to cover the cost of any unknown work.

Deeds: The documents confirming ownership of property. Also known as title deeds.

Deposit: The down payment on a property, paid when contracts are exchanged .

DG: Double-glazing.

Double skin: Two bricks that are laid side by side.

Early redemption: Paying off a loan earlier than its term.

Equity: The difference between the price of a property sold and the loan on it.

Flashing material: Usually lead, that makes external joins waterproof; for example, where a chimney meets the top of the roof.

Freehold: Ownership of a property and the land it is situated on.

FSA: The Financial Services Authority.

Full planning permission: Approval from your local authority for you to go ahead with the property improvements as indicated in the plans you have submitted to them.

Gable conservatory: A conservatory style that has a steep pitched roof giving lots of light and additional height to a conservatory.

GFCH: Gas-fired central heating.

HIP: Home Information Pack, mandatory in England and Wales from August 2007.

Hipped roof: A standard roof that slopes up on all sides to a point.

IFA: Independent financial adviser.

Infrared monitor: A monitor built into a camera so that there is still a picture at night or in low light conditions.

Interest only mortgage: A loan where you only pay the interest on the amount borrowed over the term of the mortgage.

Lantern conservatory: A period style that has two tiers with additional ceiling height in the form of a large 'lantern' shape.

Leasehold: Ownership for a set period, most commonly applied to flats and other shared buildings.

Lintel: A beam, often made of stone, that is placed above a window or door opening to support the structure.

Load bearing wall: An essential wall that is integral to the structure of a home and, if taken away, will need to be supported.

Low-e glass: Specially developed glass that helps to keep the heat in your home, provides solar heating and insulates you from noise.

Mortgage: A loan for which property is the collateral.

Mortgage protection policy: Life insurance taken out by the borrower so that the loan is paid off if they die or are sick (although policies do vary).

Mortgage redemption penalty: The charge that is sometimes made by the lender if you pay off your mortgage early.

NVQ: National Vocational or Vocations Qualification. A work-related award that is based on skills, knowledge and competence gained from studying and on-the-job training. There are various levels that can be attained.

Obelisk: A tall, thin, four-sided structure in wood or metal, used either for planting or for ornament.

Outline planning permission: An 'approval' in principle from the local authority, given subject to gaining full planning permission.

Parterre: A formally patterned flower garden, usually square or rectangular.

pH level: A measure showing the type of soil you have, such as neutral, acidic or alkaline, which helps you to understand what plants will and won't grow in your garden.

Pilkington K glass: Glass that acts both as an insulator and a conductor of solar heat to or from the home.

Planning officer: A person in the local authority who advises on changes to your property and how they might impact on nearby buildings, people and the environment.

PPI: Payment protection insurance.

PVC-U: PolyVinyl Chloride – Unplasticised; a plastic material that is used to create doors, windows, conservatories and drains.

Repayment mortgage: A loan where you pay off the interest and the sum borrowed at the same time for an agreed period.

Restrictive covenant: Legal restriction on what can be done on a property or on land.

RSJ: Rolled steel joist, added to a wall for strength.

Saracen shoot bolt: A high-security hinge that can automatically secure a window with a deadlock and further locks at the bottom and top of the frame.

SDG: Secondary double-glazing.

SVQ: The Scottish equivalent of an NVQ.

Survey: A report on the condition of a property.

Title deeds: The documents proving ownership of land.

Top-up mortgage: An additional mortgage when the first loan is not sufficient for your needs.

Variable rate: When the interest rate is not fixed and can go up or down.

Work triangle: A triangular area between the sink, cooker and refrigerator, which should be integral to a kitchen's design.

Useful addresses

Alzheimer's Society
Gordon House
10 Greencoat Place
London SW1P 1PH
Te: 020 7306 0606
www.alzheimers.org.uk

Assist UK Centres
Redbank House
4 St Chad's Street
Manchester M8 8QA
Tel: 0870 770 2866
www.assist-uk.org

Association of British Insurers
51 Gresham Street
London EC2V 7HQ
Tel: 0207 600 3333
www.abi.org.uk

Association of Plumbing and Heating
Contractors
Tel: 024 7647 0626
www.licensedplumber.co.uk

Association of Professional Landscapers
c/o The Horticultural Trades Association
19 High Street
Theale
Reding
Berkshire RG7 5AH
Tel: 0118 930 3132
www.landscaper.org.uk

Association of Project Managers
150 West Wycombe Road
High Wycombe
Buckinghamshire HP12 3AE
Tel: 0845 458 1944
www.apm.org.uk

Association of Specialist Underpinning
Contractors
Tournai Hall
Evelyn Woods Road
Aldershot
Hampshire GU11 2LL
Tel: 01252 357833
www.asuc.org.uk

Basement Information Centre
Riverside House
4 Meadows Business Park
Station Approach
Blackwater
Camberley
Surrey GU17 9AB
Tel: 01276 33155
www.basements.org.uk

British Association of Landscape
Industries
Landscape House
Stoneleigh Park
National Agricultural Centre
Warwickshire CV8 2LG
Tel: 0870 770 4971
www.bali.co.uk

British Insurance Brokers Association
14 Bevis Marks
London EC3A 7NT
Tel: 0870 950 1790
www.biba.org.uk

CADW
Welsh Assembly Government
Plas Carew
Unit 5/7 Cefn Coed
Parc Nantgarw
Cardiff CF15 7QQ
Tel: 01443 33 6000
www.cadw.wales.gov.uk

Citizens Advice Bureau (CAB)
See your local phone book or go to
www.adviceguide.org.uk

CORGI Registered
1 Elmwood
Chineham Park
Crockford Lane
Basingstoke
Hampshire RG24 8WG
Tel: 0800 9150485
www.trustcorgi.com

Council of Mortgage Lenders
Bush House
North West Wing
Aldwych
London WC2B 4PJ
Tel: 0845 373 6771
www.cml.org.uk

Designs on Property
Pear Tree House
3A Church Street
Long Bennington
Newark
Notts NG23 5EN
Tel: 0845 838 1763
www.designsonproperty.co.uk

Directgov
www.direct.gov.uk

Disabled Living Foundation
380–384 Harrow Road
London W9 2HU
Tel: 0845 130 9177
www.dlf.org.uk

Energy Savings Trust
21 Dartmouth Street,
London SW1H 9BP
Tel: 020 7222 0101
www.energysavingstrust.org.uk

English Heritage
PO Box 569
Swindon SN2 2YP
Tel: 0870 333 1181
www.english-heritage.org.uk

Environment Agency
Tel: 08708 506506
www.environment-agency.gov.uk

Federation of Master Builders
Gordon Fisher House
14–15 Great James Street
London WC1N 3DP
Tel: 020 7242 7583
www.findabuilder.co.uk

Federation of Plastering and Drywalling
Contractors
8/9 Ludgate Square
London EC4M 7AS
Tel: 020 7634 9480
www.fpdc.org

FENSA
44–48 Borough High Street
London SE1 1XB
Tel: 0870 780 2028
www.fensa.co.uk

Financial Services Authority
25 The North Colonnade
Canary Wharf
London E14 5HS
Tel: 020 7066 1000
www.fsa.gov.uk

Foundations
Bleaklow House
Howard Town Mill
Glossop
Derbyshire SK13 8HT
Tel: 01457 891909
www.foundations.uk.com

Glass and Glazing Federation
44–48 Borough High Street
London SW1 1XB
Tel: 0870 042 4255
www.ggf.co.uk

Guild of Builders and Contractors
Crest House
102–104 Church Road
Teddington
Middlesex TW11 8PY
Helpline: 020 8977 1105
www.buildersguild.co.uk

Help the Aged
207–221 Pentonville Road
London N1 9UZ
Tel: 020 7278 1114
www.helptheaged.org.uk

Historic Scotland
Longmore House
Salisbury Place
Edinburgh EH9 1SH
Tel: 0131 668 8600
www.historic-scotland.gov.uk

Institute of Carpenters
Third Floor D
Carpenters' Hall
1 Throgmorton Avenue
London EC2N 2BY
Tel: 020 7256 2700
www.carpenters-institute.org

Institute of Plumbing and Heating
Engineering
Tel: 01708 448987
www.iphe.org.uk

Landscape Institute
33 Great Portland Street
London W1W 8QG
Tel: 020 7299 4500
www.landscapeinstitute.org

Lighting Association
Stafford Park 7
Telford
Shropshire TF3 3BQ
Tel: 01952 290905
www.lightingassociation.com

Master Locksmiths Association
5d Great Central Way
Woodford Halse
Daventry
Northants NN11 3PZ
Tel: 01327 262 255
www.locksmiths.co.uk

National Federation of Builders
National Office
55 Tufton Street
London SW1P 3QL
Tel: 0870 8989 091
www.builders.org.uk

NICEIC
Warwick House
Houghton Hall Park
Houghton Regis
Dunstable
Bedfordshire LU5 5ZX
Tel: 0870 013 0382
www.niceic.org.uk

Office of Fair Trading
Fleetbank House
2–6 Salisbury Square
London EC4Y 8JX
Tel: 08457 22 44 99
www.oft.gov.uk

Painting and Decorating Association
32 Coton Road
Nuneaton
Warwickshire CV11 5TW
Tel: 024 7635 3776
www.paintingdecoratingassociation.co.uk

Planning Appeals Commission
Park House
87–91 Great Victoria Street
Belfast BT2 7AG
Tel: 028 9024 4710
www.pacni.gov.uk

The Planning Portal
G/08
Temple Quay House
2 The Square
Temple Quay
Bristol BS1 6PN
Helpdesk: 0117 372 6372
www.planningportal.gov.uk

Royal Horticultural Institute
80 Vincent Square
London SW1P 2PE
Tel: 0845 260 5000
www.rhs.org.uk

Royal Institution of Chartered Surveyors
(RICS)
RICS Contact Centre
Surveyor Court
Westwood Way
Coventry CV4 8JE
Tel: 0870 333 1600
www.rics.org.uk

Royal National Institute of the Blind
105 Judd Street
London WC1H 9NE
Tel: 020 7388 1266
www.rnib.org.uk

Royal Town Planning Institute
41 Botolph Lane
London EC3R 8DL
Tel: 020 7929 9494
www.rtpi.org.uk

Structural Waterproofing Group
1 Gleneagles House
Vernongate
Derby DE1 1UP
Tel: 01332 225100
www.structuralwaterproofing.org

Tile Association
Forum Court
83 Copers Cope Road
Beckenham
Kent BR3 1NR
Tel: 020 8663 0946
www.tiles.org.uk

Timber Research and Development Agency
Stocking Lane
Hughenden Valley
High Wycombe HP14 4ND
Tel: 01494 569600
www.trada.co.uk

Trading Standards Office
www.tradingstandards.gov.uk

Trustmark scheme
Englemere
Kings Ride
Ascot
Berkshire SL5 7TB
Tel: 08454 04 05 06
www.trustmark.org.uk

UK Kitchen Bathroom and Bedroom
Association
2 Top Barn Business Centre
Holt Heath
Worcester WR6 6NH
Tel: 01905 621787
www.kbsa.co.uk

Index

Index

219

Which? Books

Other books in this series

Buy, Sell and Move House

Kate Faulkner
ISBN: 978 1 84490 043 5
Price £10.99

Fully-updated with all the summer 2007 government changes to HIPs legislation. A complete, no-nonsense guide to negotiating the property maze and making your move as painless as possible. From dealing with estate agents to chasing solicitors, working out the true cost of your move to understanding Home Information Packs, this guide tells you how to keep things on track and avoid painful sticking points.

Buying Property Abroad

Jeremy Davies
ISBN: 978 1 84490 024 4
Price £10.99

A complete guide to the legal, financial and practical aspects of buying property abroad. This book provides down-to-earth advice on how the buying process differs from the UK, and how to negotiate contracts, commission surveys, and employ lawyers and architects. Practical tips on currency deals and taxes – and how to command the best rent – all ensure you can buy abroad with total peace of mind.

Renting and Letting

Kate Faulkner
ISBN: 978 1 84490 029 9
Price £10.99

A practical guide for landlords, tenants, and anybody considering the buy-to-let market. Covering all the legal and financial matters, including tax, record-keeping and mortgages, as well as disputes, deposits and security, this book provides comprehensive advice for anybody involved in renting property.

Which? Books

Other books in this series

Managing your Debt

Phillip Inman
ISBN: 978 1 84490 041 1
Price £10.99

Managing your Debt is a practical and straightforward guide to managing your finances and getting your money, and your life, back on track. It covers a wide range of topics including how to identify and deal with priority debts, the best way to make a debt management plan, who to write to and what to say and what to expect should you ever face bankruptcy or an individual voluntary agreement.

Making a Civil Claim

Melanie McDonald
ISBN: 978 1 84490 037 4
Price £10.99

Making a Civil Claim is the first law book in the *Essential Guides* series and is essential reading for anyone who has found him or herself in a dispute and who may be facing court or even a trial. It covers small claims as well as fast track and multi track cases and explains everything from organising your documents and making sure all the available evidence is in place, to finding the right solicitor or barrister for your case.

The Pension Handbook

Jonquil Lowe
ISBN: 978 1 84490 025 1
Price £10.99

A definitive guide to sorting out your pension, whether you're deliberating over SERPs/S2Ps, organising a personal pension or moving schemes. Cutting through confusion and dispelling apathy, Jonquil Lowe provides up-to-date advice on how to maximise your savings and provide for the future.

Which? Books

Other books in this series

Working for Yourself
Mike Pywell and Bill Hilton
ISBN: 978 1 84490 040 4
Price £10.99

Working for Yourself is a practical and straightforward guide, aimed at people who are planning the jump from a salaried, permanent contract to a freelance/entrepreneurial lifestyle. Pointing out the benefits and prospective pitfalls of being self-employed, this essential guide then details pertinent financial and legal information, as well as suggesting when and where to seek professional help.

Baby and Toddler Essentials
Anne Smith
ISBN: 978 1 84490 035 0
Price £10.99

Knowing what you need to buy when you have a child or grandchild can be a daunting business – the choice is huge, the laws are complicated and it's important to get it right. Taking each area of equipment in turn from birth to toys for your toddler, Baby and Toddler Essentials explores the goods on the market and identifies the products that might help, the products to avoid, and the essentials you really can't live without.

Giving and Inheriting
Jonquil Lowe
ISBN: 978 1 84490 032 9
Price £10.99

Inheritance tax (IHT) is becoming a major worry for more and more people. Rising house prices have pushed up the value of typical estates to a level where they are liable to be taxed at 40% on everything over £285,000. *Giving and Inheriting* is an essential guide to estate planning and tax liability, offering up-to-the–minute advice from an acknowledged financial expert, this book will help people reduce the tax bill faced by their heirs and allow many to avoid IHT altogether.

which?

[handwritten: HYSTEROSCOPY]

Which? Books

Which? Books provide impartial, expert advice on everyday matters from finance to law, property to major life events. We also publish the country's most trusted restaurant guide, *The Which? Good Food Guide*. To find out more about Which? Books, log on to www.which.co.uk or call 01903 828557.

" Which? tackles the issues that really matter to consumers and gives you the advice and active support you need to buy the right products. "